INDICTMENT

INDICTMENT

For The Murder of John F. Kennedy

The People	)	Texas Penal Code, § 15.02
V.	)	Criminal conspiracy to commit
Curtis Emerson LeMay	)	felony murder against
Lyman Louis Lemnitzer	)	John Fitzgerald Kennedy,
Defendants	)	a human being
	)	(Count 1)
	)	
	)	

Count One:

Beginning sometime in early 1963, the Defendants willfully and unlawfully carried out a conspiracy, along with like-minded individuals, named herein but not charged, to murder John F. Kennedy. The goal of this conspiracy was to supplant President John F. Kennedy with Vice-President Lyndon Baines Johnson in accordance with the succession plan prescribed by Article II, Section 1, Clause 6, of the Constitution of the United States.

J. J. Magee

authorHOUSE®

AuthorHouse™ LLC
1663 Liberty Drive
Bloomington, IN 47403
www.authorhouse.com
Phone: 1-800-839-8640

Published by AuthorHouse   10/29/2013

ISBN: 978-1-4918-0535-0 (sc)
ISBN: 978-1-4918-1842-8 (e)

Library of Congress Control Number: 2013916611

DEDICATED TO LORRAINE
MY LOVE

Contents

Preface

T his document is based on the well-established fact that there was a highly organized conspiracy at work in the killing of John F. Kennedy. Convincing evidence of this has been uncovered, not by the government agencies that should have, but by the ad hoc Grand Jury of ordinary citizens, researchers, authors, and journalists who refused to accept the patently false official story.

This posthumous indictment examines that evidence to demonstrate that the Defendants masterminded this conspiracy, reveal their motives for so doing, and show that they are guilty as charged.

The Facts of the Case

While on a political trip to Texas on November 22, 1963, President John F. Kennedy was fatally wounded at 12:30 PM while riding in an open limousine through Dealey Plaza in downtown Dallas. Texas Governor John Connally, who was seated directly in front of the President, was also seriously wounded. A description of the suspect was broadcast within fifteen minutes of the shooting. At 1:10 PM, Dallas Police Officer J. D. Tippit was shot and killed in the Oak Cliff section of the city by an unknown assailant who fled the scene on foot. Shortly thereafter, the owner of a movie theater notified police that a man fitting the description of the suspect had entered his theater without buying a ticket. A contingent of police soon arrived and at 1:50 PM arrested ex-marine Lee Harvey Oswald, an employee at the Texas School Book Depository, a building that faced Dealey Plaza. Oswald was booked for the shooting of the police officer, and was later charged with the President's assassination.

Over the course of the next two days, Oswald was moved through the Dallas police station sixteen times, and occasionally officers paused to allow him to answer questions from the media. On other occasions, he shouted back answers to questions that had been shouted to him by reporters crowding the hallway as he was paraded through the station. At every opportunity, he pronounced his innocence and requested legal representation. None was provided.

During unrecorded interrogations by Police Captain Will Fritz, Oswald denied ever owning a rifle, or purchasing one under the name 'Alek Hidell'; which was a name that appeared on a selective service card found in his wallet. At the time of his arrest, Oswald was living apart from his wife Marina. He was staying in a rented room in the Oak Cliff section of Dallas, while she was staying with Ruth Paine, a friend who owned a home in Irving. On the afternoon of November 23, Dallas police searched the Paine home, where Oswald occasionally visited his children. There in the garage, they discovered two photographs, both showed Oswald posing with a holstered pistol, a rifle in one hand, and communist literature in the other. These photographs were shown to Oswald, who according to Fritz, stated emphatically that they were fakes, that someone had superimposed his face on photographs of someone else with those guns. He told Fritz a number of times, including the Sunday morning after his arrest, that at the proper time he would prove that the pictures were phony. But, Lee Oswald never got the chance, because at 11:21 AM that same day, he was shot through a major abdominal artery by nightclub owner Jack Ruby. This happened as he was being transferred to County Jail in the basement of the Dallas police station, as millions of viewers watched on live television. Oswald was pronounced dead in Trauma Room 2 at Parkland Memorial Hospital at 1:07 PM.

In September 1964, a Presidential Commission published its findings concluding that Lee Harvey Oswald acted alone in killing the President and the Dallas Policeman, but the commission could not ascribe any one motive or group of motives to Oswald's actions. A year after these findings were published, polls showed that just forty-eight percent of Americans accepted the government's version of the assassination. The number of people who still believe that nonsense has declined to less than thirty percent today.

Opening Statement

———•———

A re we ever to know the whole truth about the violent death of the 35th President of the United States? Some years ago, it seemed certain that the facts would come to light, certainly within the lifetime of those who can remember that day. This no longer appears likely. Three out of four Americans are convinced that we will never know the truth. And, even though, in its final hours, the House Assassinations Committee hinted at a conspiracy and recommended further investigation, the reality is that there will never be another official inquiry. This is probably just as well, since the United States government has shown that it is only capable of finding that one peculiar explanation of the assassination; Lee Harvey Oswald, three shots from behind. And it becomes less credible with every passing year. Besides, memories have faded, the leads have withered, and most of the witnesses have since left this world. Nellie Connally, the last surviving occupant of the original six in the presidential limousine that day, passed away in September 2006. And for that matter, so have the Defendants and their co-conspirators, and probably the actual shooters as well.

A few of the pertinent facts we have learned from the efforts of the Grand Jury are these:

- Lee Harvey Oswald was an agent of our government who was sent on a mission to the Soviet Union as a false defector, and then returned to U.S. when that job was completed. His next assignment had him posing as the Chairman of the New Orleans Chapter of the *Fair Play for Cuba Committee*, of which he was the sole member. He worked out of the office of a private investigator by the name of Guy Banister, who was a former FBI agent with ties to a number of intelligence agencies.

- No one has ever been able to place Oswald in the corner window of the sixth floor at the time of the President's murder. Oswald told the police, according to Captain Will Fritz's notes, that when the President was shot, he was "out with Bill Shelly [the assistant manager of the Texas School Book Depository] in front." Shortly after the shooting, Book Depository Manager Roy Truly identified Oswald to a Dallas policeman in the lunchroom of the Book Depository as he drank a coke. Oswald's other claims are also true;—no sir, he did not shoot anyone, he was just a patsy.

- The President's limousine was fired on from several locations in Dealey Plaza. The first shot from the front, through the windshield and hit him in the throat. Another shot hit him in the back from the rear. He was struck in the head twice, once from the rear, and the final shot to his right temple from the right front. The shock waves of this final shot blew the President's brains out, striking Dallas Police Officer Bobby Hargis, who was riding his motorcycle to the left rear of the limousine. The impact of the blood and brain tissue hit the Officer with such force that he initially thought that he had been shot. Officer Hargis dismounted his motorcycle, drew his pistol, and charged up the grassy knoll where he was sure the shot came from, as did over eighty percent of the other eyewitnesses.

- Several Bethesda attendants saw the President's body delivered to the morgue in a cheap casket, well ahead of the bronze ceremonial casket that arrived in a the gray navy ambulance from Andrews Air Force Base with Jackie Kennedy. Before the official autopsy began, witnesses saw Dr. Humes performing clandestine post-mortem surgery extending the president's skull wound towards the front of the head in order to remove evidence of shots from the front and right front.[1]

- The ensuing autopsy was completely orchestrated by the high-ranking officers attending the procedure. The doctors assigned to perform the autopsy were not forensic pathologists, and had no experience in gunshot wounds. In fact, these doctors had been on administrative assignments and had not conducted an autopsy in several years.

Furthermore, they were told what to do, and what not to do, during the entire procedure. They were instructed to establish a cause of death only, not to establish the direction of the bullets. Why?

- Secret Service Agent Clint Hill, who climbed onto the limousine after the final shots on Elm Street, saw a large hole in the back of the President's head, as well as parts of the rear of his brain lying on the back seat of the car. The Dallas doctors also said the wound was in the rear of the president's head, yet the official autopsy photographs show the back of the President's head intact. A large piece of skull bone, identifiable as coming from the rear of a human head, was found the following day near the spot where the President was shot. Although photographs of it remain, that piece of skull bone has since disappeared. In addition, the President's brain, probably the most important piece of physical evidence in the case, is missing from the National Archives.
- A significant amount of other evidence was either tampered with, or destroyed. There are several witnesses at Parkland who saw a through-and-through bullet hole in the windshield of the limousine, and others who swear that the windshield was replaced shortly after the assassination.
- The limousine, which should have been treated as a crime scene, was wiped out as it sat parked outside Parkland Hospital's emergency entrance, and was later completely gutted and its interior replaced, on orders from LBJ.
- LBJ also had John Connally's suit and shirt sent to the dry cleaners. What explanation is there for that? Did he actually believe that the Governor was ever going to wear either of them again?

If one or two pieces of evidence in a case are lost or damaged, it may reasonably be attributed to human error. But, in this case, there is a consistent pattern where evidence which does not support the official version, is discredited, destroyed, or conveniently goes missing.

At the completion of the government's investigation, nearly all of its documentation and records were sealed away for fifty years or more. Why? If Lee Harvey Oswald was actually who the Warren Commission claimed he was, just a random 'loaner,' why would the records need to be locked away? If the government had nothing to hide, why did they hide it?

The list of suspects with purported motive to end the President's life includes Lyndon B. Johnson, the CIA, the Mafia, Anti-Castro Cubans, the FBI, and the U.S. Military. If one were to survey the literature on the assassination, they would find that for each of the suspects on the list,—with the glaring exception of the military[i]—there exists at least one treatise presenting evidence that that particular suspect had masterminded the President's murder, and convinced or coerced the others to go along. After considering a few of these you would soon realize that the Kennedy assassination is quite like the plot of Agatha Christie's 'Murder on the Orient Express;' there is credible evidence that *all* of these suspects played some role, either directly in the assassination itself, or in the cover-up afterwards. This leads to the thinking that a conspiracy which involved this many people, who would then maintain secrecy for this long, does not seem plausible. People could believe a conspiracy amongst a small number of plotters, but something that large seems a little too big to swallow.

These groups and individuals had little obvious common motive to work together for such an enormously risky endeavor as eliminating the President of the United States. Although each had their own specific reasons for wanting JFK out of office, to have this diverse group come together for the assassination and its cover-up there would need to be a single common unifying purpose. What possible motive would be important enough to have them put their normal intermural squabbling aside and compelling enough to have them maintain perpetual silence?

---

[i] There a few which consider retired members of the military, but none that examine those on active duty.

Military:

Considering the hierarchy of the suspects, it is apparent that masterminding the assassination could only be done by one group on that list, and logically that would be the military. It is highly unlikely that the military would accept taking direction from any of the other suspects on the list for an operation as serious as this one. Recall that in 1960 the men in charge at the Pentagon were the officers who moved up the ranks after simultaneously defeating Germany and Japan. And, in the post-war environment, they wielded incredible clout, especially now that there was a new enemy for them to protect America from: international communism.

Note also that they were involved in every key aspect of the assassination. They controlled significant portions of the President's protection, or in this case, the lack thereof. They maintained custody of the President's body afterward, refusing to permit JFK's entourage to carry the coffin off Air Force One when it returned to Washington. They also had complete control of the autopsy, where many of the highest-ranking officers were in attendance directing the entire procedure. Why did they want the President dead? Their motives for his murder will be presented herein.

The Un-indicted Co-conspirators

The following individuals and/or organizations participated in either the assassination or its cover-up, and in some cases both. Their roles in the assassination are further described herein and are presented to show the overall scope of the plot. However, as will be shown, the plot originated with the Defendants who enlisted the assistance of these others in carrying it out.

Lyndon Baines Johnson:

If the purpose of a coup d'état is to change policy by changing leader, then if the vice president had been a JFK loyalist, the assassination would have been pointless. But afterward, Johnson, claiming all the while to be following JFK's policies, actually pursued policies decidedly different from Kennedy. These policy changes were, in nearly all aspects, more in line with what the military wanted. Johnson's participation in the plot is credible because, as is well known, he had considerable presidential ambitions of his own, and had only narrowly lost the Democratic nomination to JFK in 1960. In fact, the only reason Johnson accepted the second position on the Democratic ticket in the first place was the possibility of succession:

> Clare Boothe Luce and Lyndon Johnson sit together on a bus which will take them to one of the many inaugural balls during the evening. Luce asks Johnson why he ever took the Vice-Presidency. Johnson answers: "Clare, I looked it up; one out of every four presidents has died in office. I'm a gamblin' man, darlin', and this is the only chance I got."[2]

And in late 1963, he had even more incentive to help with the plot. Johnson by that time had been linked to two serious and separate investigations. The first involved the suspicious death of an Agricultural Adjustment Administration employee named Henry Marshall, who had been investigating the misappropriation of cotton allotment funds by Billie Sol Estes, a businessman with direct ties to LBJ. The second was an emerging scandal involving influence peddling through Senate Majority Secretary Bobby Baker, who also had close ties to Johnson and was then under investigation by Attorney General Robert Kennedy. The word in the Democratic Party was that Johnson would not be on the '64 ticket, and would probably go to prison.

The Dallas trip was announced in September 1963. LBJ played a major role in its planning; after all, it was his home state. And those planning the assassination would want to fill-in the successor ahead of time, although he may not have been fully informed on all of the details. Johnson displayed exactly such advanced knowledge in at least two instances.

The first was revealed by Johnson's mistress, Ms. Madeleine Brown, who related that on the night before the assassination, Johnson told her, two different times, that," . . . after tomorrow, those goddamn

Kennedys will never embarrass me again. That's no threat; that's a promise." The second occurred when Johnson went to JFK's hotel suite in Fort Worth on Thursday evening where the two men got into an argument that could be heard by the hotel staff outside in the hallway. Reportedly, they fought about Johnson's demand to change the seating arrangements in the cars for the next morning's motorcade in Dallas. In a clear breach of protocol, Johnson was insisting that, Governor Connally (his good friend) ride with him and that Senator Yarborough (his political enemy) ride in the presidential limousine with JFK. The president flatly refused, and Johnson stormed off in a fit of rage.[3] Johnson was clearly trying to protect his friend from the shooting.

JFK's death the next day simultaneously made all of Johnson's problems miraculously disappear, and his presidential aspirations come true. It is not surprising then that 'Lyndon' was the name at the top of the list of suspects that Kennedy's personal secretary wrote down during the long and mournful flight back to Washington on Air Force One.

Central Intelligence Agency:

This agency, created as part of the National Security Act of 1947, was formed from various separate military intelligence groups such as the OSS. It was intended to operate at the direction of the National Security Council, which placed the origin of covert operations at the top level of government. But, as time went on, and administration personnel changed, whereas the CIA's did not, the tail was soon wagging the dog as the CIA independently developed plans of its own and passed them up, instead of the other way around. After one of their major operations, the planned overthrow of Fidel Castro using Cuban exiles, turned out to be a complete failure, JFK vowed to dismantle the CIA. The Agency had a major reason to have the President removed, its own preservation.

In the pecking order, the military considered the CIA as secondary to themselves and viewed the Agency as a support organization. It is also highly unlikely that the CIA could have decided that the President had to be eliminated on their own volition. There is substantial evidence that the CIA actually carried out the assassination, but did so under the sponsorship and direction of the military.

New Orleans District Attorney Jim Garrison is the only person to bring a trial against anyone in the death of the President. Garrison prosecuted businessman Clay Shaw, charging that he was a CIA operative who worked with former FBI agent Guy Banister as part of the conspiracy that killed the President. Anti-communist Banister fronted a private detective agency, out of which Lee Harvey Oswald handed out pro-Communist "Fair Play for Cuba" leaflets. Once Garrison's investigation became public, many of his key witnesses suddenly died, committed 'suicide', or were killed just before the trial, and Clay Shaw was found not guilty. Years later, the CIA admitted that Shaw was in fact a CIA agent. Although Garrison was derided in the media, his efforts refocused attention on the case and his work is responsible for the release of the Zapruder film to the public.

Mafia & Anti-Castro Cubans:

The mafia and anti-Castro Cuban groups were a tier below the CIA, so it is even less likely that they could have ordered the assassination and persuaded both the CIA and the military to cooperate. But their contact with the CIA in anti-Castro activities likely gave them advanced information, which would explain why some of their members also displayed foreknowledge of JFK's death.

FBI:

Director J. Edgar Hoover despised the Kennedy brothers and feared that the Kennedys would replace him as FBI director, but he did not have the means to carry out an assassination on his own. Although, as an accessory after the fact, Hoover provided significant help to Johnson and the Warren Commission in focusing the investigation on Oswald and ignoring all else.

The Defendants

The Joint Chiefs of Staff (JCS) system of Military leadership was still relatively new to the U.S. armed forces in the early 1960's. It was modeled after the British Chiefs of Staff Committee system when it began in 1942 as the 'Unified High Command.' It was formed to coordinate the war effort with England, during which, the JCS steadily grew in influence and was subsequently established formally by President Truman as part of the same National Security Act that created the National Security Council and the CIA. The particular members of the Joint Chiefs at the Pentagon at the time of the Kennedy administration had served under its first members during the war. Its most prominent members were:

General Lyman Louis Lemnitzer Chairman, a West Point graduate who served in the Philippines and was later assigned to General Eisenhower's staff. He helped plan the invasions of North Africa and Sicily. After the war, he was assigned to the Strategic Survey Committee of the Joint Chiefs of Staff. Lemnitzer was named Chief of Staff of the Army in 1957 and appointed Chairman September 1960.

General Curtis Emerson LeMay in 1957 was made Vice Chief, and in 1960 promoted to Chief of Staff of the Air Force. He had been a bomber pilot in the Army Air Corps prior to creation of the Air Force. He participated in both war theaters. In Europe, he was part of the Eighth Air Force and led it in combat until May 1943. He was, without question, one of the most courageous commanders in any branch of the military. He often demonstrated this by personally piloting the lead plane on the most dangerous bombing missions. Later in the Pacific, he implemented a systematic strategic fire bombing campaign against Japan's cities. And it was his bomb group that dropped the atomic bombs on Hiroshima and Nagasaki. After the war, he headed the Berlin airlift, and later reorganized the Strategic Air Command (SAC) into a fearsome weapon of nuclear war.

However, General Maxwell Taylor thought it was a mistake to promote LeMay to this position, believing that a good bomber commander does not necessarily make a good Chief of Staff.

> Meetings of the Joint Chiefs of Staff were alluded to by some as a three-ring circus. General Curtis E. LeMay, Air Force chief of staff, was characterized by one observer as always injecting himself into situations "like a rogue elephant barging out of a forest." There are many stories of LeMay's crudeness in dealing with his colleagues on the Joint Chiefs of Staff. He found the meetings dull, tiring, and unproductive. Petulant and often childish when he didn't get his way, LeMay would light a cigar and blow smoke in the direction of anyone challenging his position. To show utter disgust, he would walk into the private Joint Chiefs of Staff toilet, leave the door open, urinate or break wind loudly, and flush the commode a number of aggravating times. He would then saunter calmly back into the meeting pretending that nothing had happened. When angry with individual staff members, he would resort to sarcasm; if that failed, he would direct his wrath to the entire staff. [4]

Mens Rea[ii]

——•——

To understand the actions of the military chiefs, and the Defendants specifically, it is necessary to examine their recent experience, and establish how their collective state of mind turned criminal during the Kennedy administration. Each had fought and distinguished himself in World War II, the war against Fascism. In the fifteen years after that war ended, they had been engaged in a new kind of war. They fought strategic battles with their new enemy, in constant preparation for the ultimate war to come. This was to be the war against communism. For the Defendants and their associates, this was every bit as real as an actual war; it was just that the shooting had not started yet. These men had become the country's first line of defense against the communist menace. Over the next several pages, a summary of the evolution their state of mind from the Second World War to the early 1960's is presented. This will establish a basis to show why they saw JFK as a threat that had to be eliminated.

World War II

Over the decade following World War I, which was once known as 'the war to end all wars,' a former German Army lance corporal named Adolph Hitler formed the National Socialist (NAZI) Party, which he used to wrest control of that country in 1933, and then promptly set about undoing the humiliating Treaty of Versailles. As Germany spiraled into debt in the Great Depression, Hitler reneged on reparation payments and instead began to re-arm his country in direct violation of that treaty and to re-acquire the territories that Germany had been forced to surrender. In 1938, he demanded German annexation of part of Czechoslovakia known as the

---

ii   Literally 'Guilty Mind': a person's awareness that his or her conduct is criminal

Sudetenland, under the pretext of protecting its largely Germanic population. In the interest of averting war, Prime Ministers Neville Chamberlain of Great Britain and Édouard Daladier of France, (notably without a representative from Czechoslovakia) caved into Hitler's demands on September 30, 1938 by agreeing to a deal where, in exchange for the Sudetenland, Hitler promised to not seek any further territory. This strategy became known as *Appeasement*. On his return to Britain, Chamberlain delivered his infamous speech standing on the tarmac, waving the single scrap of paper signed by Hitler, proclaiming that the agreement reached in Munich had assured "peace for our time."

The first indication that their Appeasement policy was an utter failure, however, came six months later, when Hitler took over the rest of the country, completely unopposed. He was able to do this by inviting the elderly Czech President to Berlin, and then holding him hostage until he signed over the whole country. With an invitation approved by the Czech President, the British and French could do little.

On September 1, 1939, just eleven months after the Munich Agreement, Hitler invaded Poland. Two days later Britain, France, Australia and New Zealand declared war on Germany. The Second World War had begun. That night, President Roosevelt gave one of his trademark 'fireside chat' radio broadcasts in which he reaffirmed his commitment to keep America out of the war, while at the same time announcing his intention to repeal the arms embargo against Britain. But public opposition quickly sprang up to any modification of the Neutrality Act, supported by notable Americans such as 31st President Herbert Hoover and aviation hero Charles Lindbergh. The 32nd President's apparent isolationist remarks, along with the opposition to revising the Neutrality Act served to reinforce Japan's belief that the United States would not fight.

After Denmark and Norway were forced to surrender to Germany in April 1940, Neville Chamberlain and his Appeasement government were forced to resign. In May, Nazi mechanized divisions rolled through the Netherlands, Belgium, and Luxembourg on their way through France, forcing the retreat of French and British Armies to Dunkirk, where they had to be evacuated across the English Channel. France surrendered on June 22, and Britain's First Lord of the Admiralty, Winston Churchill, who had railed against Chamberlain's Appeasement Policies, now became Britain's Prime Minister.

Throughout his public life, Neville Chamberlain had been renowned for always carrying a large umbrella wherever he went, rain or shine. He was so identified with this particular inclement weather accessory, in fact, that after the calamitous outcome of his abject capitulation in the Munich Agreement, his trademark LARGE BLACK UMBRELLA forever after became the universal iconic symbol of Appeasement itself.

A little more than a year after war broke out in Europe, the nation of Japan decided to launch a pre-emptive attack on the American Fleet at Pearl Harbor, in order to prevent American interference with its plans for conquest in Asia, particularly its ongoing invasion of China. Their decision to attack had been preceded by a decade of increasing tensions between the two nations. These had peaked most recently because of a U.S. embargo of oil and scrap metal exports to Japan, after Japan's invasion of French Indochina. The Japanese believed that the U.S. was unprepared for war and, judging by its fractured and predominately isolationist public discourse was unwilling to fight. The Japanese concluded that destroying its pacific fleet would decide the issue by rendering the U.S. incapable of fighting. Their attack on Hawaii was scheduled to occur immediately after the Japanese Ambassador had delivered a warning to Washington. However, the Japanese Embassy's difficulties in translating the coded message from Tokyo caused a delay in its delivery until after the bombing. The then 'surprise attack' caused such public outrage that the isolationist discourse vanished as FDR requested, and received, a declaration of war the next day. Germany and Italy reciprocated by declaring war on the U.S. on the 11th.

One month prior to Germany's invasion of Poland, at the urging of fellow scientists, eminent physicist and Nobel laureate, Albert Einstein, signed a letter to United States President Franklin Delano Roosevelt, advising him of powerful new weapons that may be possible using a certain isotope of uranium. The letter then went on to state its main purpose: to warn the American President that there was convincing evidence that German scientists may already be working for the Nazis in this effort. Roosevelt formed *The Uranium Committee* to look into nuclear research, but the work was slow to start. It gained momentum after the British MAUD committee showed that such a weapon would require only a few pounds of fissionable material, and intelligence reports indicated that the Germans had begun hoarding uranium supplies. Roosevelt approved the project in early December 1941, as the Japanese fleet closed in on Hawaii. After the U.S. entry into the war, the project was taken over by Vannevar Bush, the director of the Office of Scientific Research and Development, who assigned it to the Manhattan Engineer District of the Army Corps of Engineers. In what became known as the *Manhattan Project*, the United States government embarked on a crash program whose sole purpose was to develop an atomic bomb. Because it could very well decide the outcome of the war, this project was given the highest priority, and no amount of effort or expense was spared towards the achievement of its goal.

Following the Nazi surrender in May 1945, the allies discovered that even though German scientists had seen the potential for nuclear weapons, by the end of the war, they had made surprisingly little progress towards that objective. Conversely, the Americans, in cooperation with the British and the Canadians, motivated by the terrifying prospect of an atomic bomb in the hands of the Germans, had conquered the formidable technological problems. At 5:30 AM on July 16, 1945, in the New Mexico desert near Alamogordo, the Manhattan Project team detonated the world's first nuclear explosion. Witnessing the successful test, code-named *TRINITY*, J. Robert Oppenheimer, the project's scientific director, recalled a passage from the Hindu scripture, the *Bhagavad-Gita*,

Now I am become Death, the destroyer of worlds.[5]

For the inhabitants of the Japanese city of Hiroshima, the world was destroyed on the morning of August 6, by a single atomic bomb. Three days later Nagasaki was similarly obliterated. Japan surrendered on August 14.

The war that began with the German invasion of Poland, officially ended six years later with the formal surrender of Japan on September 2, 1945 aboard the American battleship, *Missouri*, anchored in Tokyo Bay. All tolled, the war took the lives of an estimated fifty-two million people worldwide. Afterward, American troops occupied Japan, while Germany was occupied by Allied forces. But, the Allies were now divided into East and West, with the US, Brittan and France in the West, and the Soviet Union in the East. Germany was likewise divided, and its capitol, Berlin, located entirely in the Russian zone, was likewise split into East and West sectors. As part of the four-party agreement, the West was understood to have permanent access rights through East Germany to their sectors of Berlin. Just as after WWI, the end of one conflict set the stage for future ones.

Cold War

After all of its previous wars, the United States disbanded its armies, sent the troops home, and American citizens resumed their normal lives. Based on the sage advice of George Washington, 'normal life' usually meant staunch isolationism. However, the America that emerged from World War II was a very different country from the one that entered it; isolationism was over. And completely disbanding the armies this time was out of the question because they were needed to occupy and rebuild Europe and Japan.

In this post-war world, the United States now had a monumental choice to make. The American government, at unprecedented effort and expense, had successfully produced the most powerful weapon yet devised by man. And now that the war that caused its creation was over, a decision needed to be made as to how this new discovery should be handled. While many in the military considered it no different from any other bomb, bullet, or grenade, many others in the government recognized the significant effect it would have on relations among the nations of the world. The U.S. could either share this technology with its allies and thereby establish mutual controls, or, presuming that no one else would be able to develop nuclear weapons on their own, attempt to extend its monopoly indefinitely.

In light of this pending decision, were the Soviets, who played a major role in the defeat of Germany, still to be considered as one of our Allies? Suspicion of the Soviet Union went back to the communist revolution in which the West had supported the Czar, and had only deepened because of the Second World War. At the beginning of that conflict, Stalin formed a non-aggression pact with Hitler and simultaneously invaded Poland's eastern border when the Nazis invaded its western. This was followed by the Soviet's invasions of Latvia, Estonia, Lithuania, and Finland. Our alliance with the Soviets began only after Hitler double-crossed Stalin and attacked Russia, making the Germans our common enemy. Five years later, with the defeat of Germany in sight, President Franklin Roosevelt, British Prime Minister Winston Churchill, and Soviet Premier Joseph Stalin met at a conference in Yalta to decide arrangements for the post-war world. The Yalta Agreement established that after the war, European governments would be chosen by free elections. Except that, Roosevelt and Churchill agreed to Stalin's insistence that the new Polish government would be one 'agreeable to the Soviet Union.' Apparently, neither western leader understood exactly what Stalin meant by 'agreeable.'

Whatever relationship had developed during the war changed dramatically when Roosevelt suddenly died in April 1945; only a month prior to the German surrender. Shortly thereafter, Churchill was replaced as British Prime Minister. And instead of free elections, Stalin was installing communist governments 'agreeable to the Soviet Union' in Eastern Europe, which was perceived as reneging on his Yalta agreements. FDR had kept his fourth Vice President, Harry Truman, completely uninformed regarding any of the details concerning American Foreign affairs. But now, only twelve days into his sudden presidency, Truman held his first meeting with a representative of the Soviet Union, Foreign Minister Vyacheslav Molotov. Anxious to demonstrate his own toughness, Truman took a hard line approach, upbraiding Molotov about Russia's post-war actions in Eastern Europe.

> 'I have never been talked to like that in my life,' protested Molotov. 'Carry out your agreements, and you won't get talked to like that,' snapped Truman.[6] And in [Andrei] Gromoyko's account: 'Quite unexpectedly, still in the middle of our talk, Truman suddenly half rose and gave a sign to indicate that our conversation was over, in effect breaking off the meeting.' [7]

Later, Gromokyo believed that Truman's belligerent behavior was due to his knowledge of the atom bomb. It was not. Truman was not informed about the Manhattan Project until two days after that meeting.[8]

After his tutoring on *the* bomb, while in route to the Potsdam Conference in July, a coded message was passed to the 33[rd]President, letting him know that the *TRINITY* test had been a success. So, later during the conference, Truman, found an opportunity to casually inform Stalin about America's 'powerful new weapon.' Truman noted in his diary that the Soviet leader appeared completely unimpressed, from which he concluded that Stalin did not comprehend the power of the atomic bomb. The truth was quite the opposite, because the Soviet Premier had known all about the American nuclear weapons program and long before Harry Truman did. Since nearly the beginning of the Manhattan Project, spies in the weapons lab at Los Alamos had been smuggling secrets to the Soviets, who used them to develop a nuclear program of their own. Stalin's awareness that his 'Allies' had been keeping him in the dark about this weapon garnered reciprocal suspicion and mistrust, leading the Soviet Premier to interpret the new American president's revelation, following his recent confrontation with Molotov, as a direct threat.

Relations between the US and the Soviet Union steadily deteriorated. In June 1948, as part of Europe's economic recovery plan, the western allies' decided to introduce a new currency in the allied sections of Germany. The allies wanted to accelerate Germany's recovery in order to free themselves from the huge financial burden and to avoid repeating the mistakes of the First World War. The Russians, however, very definitely wanted to stifle German economic recovery because for them, each time the Germans prospered, war followed. Concerned about the effects of the new monetary policy in their sectors, East German border guards attempted to stop western vehicles to search for the verboten currency, a search that the British, French and Americans refused. The Soviets responded by blocking western road and rail access to East Berlin. Thus began the 'Berlin Blockade.' General Lucius Clay, the American magistrate in Berlin, requested the Air Force to fly-in a supply of coal. The Air Force, under General LeMay, responded by converting every available transport plane for around-the-clock food and fuel supply flights into West Berlin.

In September of that very tense period, the National Security Council issued NSC-030, *"United States Policy On Nuclear Warfare,"* which ordered the military, particularly the Strategic Air Command, to "utilize promptly and effectively all appropriate means available, including atomic weapons, in the interest of National Security, . . . [and to] . . . plan accordingly." This gave LeMay license to do whatever he believed was necessary, so he moved a Group of B-29's from the U.S. to England as an unambiguous message to the Soviets that we would attack with atomic weapons if they interfered with the airlift. At the beginning of the crisis, LeMay proposed to General Clay that he march a Column of soldiers down the autobahn and if there were any interference from the Russians, LeMay would respond by bombing Soviet planes on the runway at their base in East Germany. Clay declined. The crisis did not abate until the following May when the Soviets relented and reopened western access.

The U.S. was stunned that same September 1948, when an American reconnaissance plane detected radioactive particulate in the atmosphere in the North Pacific just outside Soviet airspace. The plutonium isotope they found provided proof that the Soviet Union had detonated an atomic weapon, and many years before American intelligence believed they could. It took several weeks to convince

Truman of the fact, who finally made a public announcement. Stalin did not confirm the Soviet A-bomb until a few weeks after Truman's announcement, for fear of an American attack on his nuclear facilities. This grim news was nearly simultaneous with the proclamation of the Communist Revolution in China's final victory over Nationalist Chiang Kai-shek. The combined effect contributed significantly to the rising sense that the communists were encircling the free world in furtherance of their overall plan.

A consequence of the Japanese surrender ending World War II was that it also ended their forty-year occupation of Korea. The peninsula was subsequently divided at the 38th parallel under a United Nations Trusteeship, with a western aligned South and a communist aligned North. Each half was determined to conquer the other. In June 1949, American troops were withdrawn from Korea, and in an address by Secretary of State Acheson to the National Press Club in mid-January 1950, Korea was not included as one of the countries that America would defend. The Secretary's speech led Stalin to conclude that America would not intervene on the peninsula and so he approved North Korea's incessant request to attack the south.

On June 25, North Korean forces stormed across the 38th parallel, initiating the first major armed conflict of the Cold War. Caught off guard, United Nations troops suffered early defeats. Truman sent in US troops but rejected a request from LeMay "to turn SAC loose with incendiaries" on North Korea. Douglas MacArthur led a successful counter-offensive with a daring amphibious landing behind enemy lines at Inchon, and drove the North Koreans back.

The United States was convinced that Stalin had masterminded the attack as part of his overall plan for world domination. The Air Force moved two B-29 Groups to Japan in preparation for a nuclear attack against China and an anticipated general war with the Soviet Union. Not only had Washington not approved this war plan, they had never even seen it; these actions were exclusively the decisions of SAC commander LeMay, who refused to submit his plan for approval because, he said, submitting it to Washington would jeopardize its security.

Chinese warnings of intervention if U.N. forces came across the 38th parallel into North Korea were ignored, as MacArthur had secretly been given authority by Secretary of Defense George Marshall to take over the entire peninsula, so he pushed North toward the Chinese border on the Yalu River. When he did, the Communist Chinese made good on their threat and came to the aid of the North Koreans en masse, sweeping the U.N. forces back below the 38th parallel. It was the worst retreat in the two hundred years of American military history. In full retreat, MacArthur demanded permission to use nuclear weapons against China, otherwise, he warned, the peninsula would have to be evacuated. Truman would not allow MacArthur free reign to conduct the war as he wished, or expand it into China, after which the President's relationship with his Generals became intensely strained.

Per his request, the Joint Chiefs of Staff drafted orders for MacArthur, authorizing him to use nuclear weapons to attack air bases in China. However, Truman would not approve these orders, and because of MacArthur's blatant insubordination, the 33rd President relieved him of command on April 10, replacing him with General Matthew Ridgeway. The Korean conflict then transitioned into a protracted World War I style war of attrition that outlasted the Truman administration.

Even though he was not permitted to firebomb North Korea immediately, the way he wanted to, LeMay eventually destroyed a large number of North Korean cities "piecemeal."[9]

> So we went over there and fought the war and eventually burned down every town in North Korea anyway, some way or another, and some in South Korea too. We even burned down Pusan—an accident but we burned it down anyway . . . Over a period of three years or so we killed off—what—twenty percent of the population of Korea as direct casualties of war, or from starvation and exposure?[iii] Over a period of three years this seemed to be acceptable to

---

[iii] Totaling 4,525,000 Korean deaths, North and South, civilian and military (op. cit.).

everybody, but to kill a few people at the start right away, no
we can't seem to stomach that.

Beginning with the firebombing of Tokyo, to the atomic bombing
of Hiroshima and Nagasaki, and now the firebombing of Korea, the
military in general, and LeMay in particular, had become completely
desensitized to the mass killing of large civilian populations. Nuclear
weapons now made that objective more efficient.

Once the Soviets had the atomic bomb, Truman approved the
development of the 'Super', the hydrogen bomb, which was completed
in late 1952. Unlike fission weapons, this more powerful fusion bomb
was not limited in size. Many scientists opposed its development
because there were no military targets large enough to warrant its
use, and it would only be used against civilians. In one of his last
acts as president, Truman approved the first H-bomb test, which
was code-named *MIKE*. The test was carried out on Elugelab, part
of the Enewetak Atoll, on November 1, 1952, just days before the
presidential election. The small island of Elugelab disappeared in the
ten-megaton explosion.

The newly inaugurated 34th President, Dwight D. Eisenhower, and
his staunch anti-communist Secretary of State, John Foster Dulles,
decided to take a more militant stand against the communists than
the previous administration. Eisenhower began with the stalemate in
Korea where he let the Soviets, the Koreans, and the Chinese know
that he was prepared to use nuclear weapons to end the war. The
legend has been that this threat forced the Chinese into an armistice,
but in reality, their sudden change in attitude had more to do with
the death of Joseph Stalin, after which the communists were anxious
to end the war. An armistice was signed in 1953 and the border
was restored to the 38th Parallel. A peace treaty was never signed,
however, so theoretically, a state of war still exists. At a human cost
well exceeding five million lives, the first battle of the Cold War ended
exactly where it began.

Eisenhower subscribed to the idea that nuclear bombs were no
different from any other weapon of war, and never expressed any

qualms about their use, as Truman had after Japan. In fact, he transferred control of ninety-percent of these weapons from the Atomic Energy Commission (AEC) directly to the military. And, he actually welcomed the new thermonuclear weapons because they were less expensive than fission weapons, and much less expensive than maintaining a large conventional force. And now, with the budget responsibility of his new office, he stressed the Air Force as the nation's major deterrent, and focusing on thermonuclear weapons allowed him to do both. This emphasis on the Bomber Force was referred to as the 'New Look' of the American military, which relied on the principle of massive retaliation to threats posed by communist nations.

Less than a year after the *MIKE* test, this new weapon was countered by the Soviet version of the H-bomb, which they tested on August 12, 1953. Now both sides began stockpiling these much more powerful nuclear weapons, so the strategic situation had radically changed. A surprise attack now would leave a country no time to ramp up for war. The next major conflict would destroy an unprepared nation in a matter of days, and possibly only hours.

The belief that the communists were plotting world conquest, and that they were building a nuclear arsenal to accomplish that goal, in combination with the memory of the Japanese surprise attack on Pearl Harbor, led the military to conduct serious studies for launching a preventative war. In 1953 an Air Force Study entitled "*The Coming National Crisis*" recommended to President Eisenhower that he precipitate a war with the U.S.S.R., and soon, before the enemy achieved a nuclear capability large enough to threaten the United States.[10] Eisenhower rejected the plan, pronouncing that the United States and its allies would never initiate a war.

But Eisenhower worried constantly about a surprise attack, so he permitted SAC to plan for a pre-emptive strike, which would be initiated if it were determined that the Russians were about to launch a sneak attack against the United States. SAC Commander LeMay, who considered every day as though it was the day before the next war, transformed the U.S. capability to launch a pre-emptive strike to ultra-high readiness. There were planes in the air around the clock with command and control capable of ordering a U.S. nuclear strike in case Washington had already been destroyed. He timed the U.S. attack so that SAC bombers would arrive at the Russian border at a large number of locations simultaneously, thereby overwhelming Soviet defenses. According to a navy Captain who attended a SAC briefing at Offutt Air Force base in March 1954, LeMay told the attendants that if all went according to plan, the Soviet Union would be a "smoking radiating ruin at the end of two hours."[11]

To plan this attack, the military needed up to date information on both Soviet defensive and offensive capability. In the days before satellites, the U.S. used spy planes to gather this information, starting with modified bombers flying around the perimeter of the U.S.S.R. Later in the 1950s, with ever faster and higher flying aircraft, LeMay had American reconnaissance planes flying directly over the Soviet Union. Soon U.S. advances in aircraft exceeded the Russian's ability to shoot them down, and planes flew over Soviet airspace unopposed. In 1956, the first U-2 flight crossed over the USSR. This ultrahigh altitude spy plane flew well beyond the capability of Soviet jets to intercept them.

However, the intelligence information they collected was still relatively incomplete so the rest was extrapolated. The result was that U.S. estimates of Russian capability were highly overstated, translating into huge increases in American armaments. The number of nuclear weapons in the U.S. arsenal went from 300 in 1950, to 1,300 in 1953, and to 18,000 by 1960.

LeMay also used these overflights to test Soviet air defenses, which could well have escalated into war. There is some evidence that he wanted to do exactly that; provoke the Russians into responding to these flights so that he could justify his pre-emptive assault. After one mission he told the crew that "if we do these overflights right, maybe we can get World War III started." He, more than anyone, wanted to use the American advantage before the Russians could catch up, as he later lamented, "That was the era when we might have destroyed Russia completely and not even skinned our elbows doing it."

The SAC commander was achieving his intended purpose. The Russians were becoming increasingly incensed about U.S. overflights. But, since they could not do too much about them, they did not say too much about them publically. That is, until they shot down and captured U-2 Pilot Francis Gary Powers. Khrushchev announced the shooting down of the American plane, but concealed the fact that the pilot survived until he trapped Eisenhower in the cover story, (that is to say lie) that it was a weather plane that had strayed off-course. Khrushchev then produced a live pilot who admitted that he had been spying. This coincidently occurred just as a scheduled summit in Paris between Khrushchev and Eisenhower began. When Eisenhower refused to apologize for the U-2 Incident, Khrushchev cancelled the summit. After then-Senator John Kennedy stated that Eisenhower should have expressed regret about the incident, Kennedy was immediately accused of appeasement[12]. Powers himself said that someone had to have given the Soviets secret information to shoot down his U-2, and later even suggested that it may have been a defector named Lee Oswald, who had been stationed at Atsugi AFB in Japan where U-2 flights took off.

In 1957, Eisenhower formed a committee to evaluate a recommendation from the Federal Civil Defense Administration (FCDA) that the federal government spend approximately thirty billion dollars over the next seven years on construction of bomb and fallout shelters. This committee, known as "the Gaither Committee" expanded their work into an overall evaluation of National Security and preparedness. When SAC Commander LeMay was interviewed by the committee, he admitted that he could not respond in time to a warning that soviet planes were at the DEW[iv] line, but he stated that he was not going to wait for a warning that the Russians were on their way to attack the United States. He revealed that he was spying on the Soviets all the time and if he saw them preparing to attack, he would order a pre-emptive strike to, "knock the shit out of them while they were still on the ground." When the committee chairman

---

[iv] DEW was the Distant Early Warning Line of radar detection around the North Pole.

pointed out, "but General LeMay, that's not national Policy." LeMay replied, "I don't care. It's *my* policy. That's what *I'm* going to do."[13] The committee did not mention this stark exchange in its report.

On October 4, 1957, just as the Gaither Committee was preparing that final report, the Soviet Union launched the world's first artificial satellite into space. It was a 23-inch diameter, 185-pound metal ball that the Russians named 'Sputnik,' which orbited the planet every hour and a half, constantly transmitting signals back to earth. The clear implication was that the Soviets were ahead of the U.S. in rocket technology and that they could use it to deliver nuclear weapons anywhere in the world. Europeans now wondered if the Americans would still come to their aid if Russian ICBMs threatened the U.S. The Soviet achievement occurred at the same time United States' attempts to launch intercontinental range rockets failed, with several exploding on their launch pads. The issuance of the Top Secret Gaither report on November 7, entitled *"Deterrence and Survival in the Nuclear Age,"* raised alarms in Washington regarding the vulnerability of our nuclear arsenal to surprise attack. The report was leaked to reporter Chalmers Roberts[14] of the Washington Post, who wrote that the United States was, "in the gravest danger in its history" because the Soviets were out-pacing us in weapons production, and that no defense would ever be sufficient to assure our survival. Three committee members privately recommend launching a pre-emptive war. These two near simultaneous events spawned what came to be known as the 'Missile Gap,' the perception that the U.S. was behind the Soviet Union in nuclear weapons. Massachusetts Senator Kennedy delivered a speech on the senate floor blaming Eisenhower's budget cuts for allowing America to fall behind. "We have selected a defense that meets our budget needs, instead of the other way around." Khrushchev took full advantage of American fears by deceitfully boasting that the Soviet Union was turning out missiles 'like sausages.' Public concern approached panic levels.

Based on U-2 over flights, Eisenhower knew, but could not reveal, that he had first-hand knowledge that the Missile Gap was complete fiction, and that the Gaither Report had grossly overestimated Soviet capability. The President was under intense pressure to do something but was unable to disclose the truth. He was also concerned that if he made public denials of a missile gap, it would only drive the Soviets to increase production. So, instead, Eisenhower decided to follow through with nearly all of the Gaither Committee's recommendations, including one to strengthen our nuclear deterrent by installing American Intermediate Range Ballistic Missiles (IRBMs) in Europe. He convinced NATO allies Italy and Turkey to accept U.S. Jupiter missiles, in spite of the fact that he considered these liquid-fueled models to be worth little more than scrap metal. Furthermore, he decided to go ahead with this plan fully aware that the Soviet Union would consider the missile installation near their border ". . . a provocative step analogous to the deployment of Soviet missiles in Mexico or Cuba."[15] The missiles in Turkey would not become operational until April 1962.

The America of the late 1950's

The United States and the Soviet Union both entered the Second World War as the result of a surprise attack on their home soil: we by the Japanese, and they by the Germans. But, we considered their case different from ours since they had been the allies of the Nazis prior to Hitler's double-cross. And now, we both suffered from what Herman Kahn termed "the mutual fear of surprise attack, where each side imputes to the other aggressive intentions and misreads purely defensive preparations as being offensive."[16]

The mere possibility of an atomic bomb in the hands of the Third Reich drove us into a frantic program to develop our own. After our success, we, perhaps without actually intending to, presented the Soviet Union with the exact stark horror that had loomed over us; a potential adversary armed with weapons for which there could be no defense. When they reacted with the same survival instinct that had driven us, we denounced them as seeking world domination. The Soviets were certainly not without blame for the cold war, but on the other hand, neither were they the bloodthirsty monsters that we made them. We magnified the Soviet Menace and distorted the threat far beyond their actual capabilities.

Once they too had nuclear weapons, our military concluded that war with the Soviet Union was unavoidable. And, based on that assumption, their reasoning progressed that we should start a war now, while we have the means to win decisively, and still had personnel with the will to carry it out. Rather than let communism fester the way fascism did in the 1930's we should rid the world of it now, before its followers could out-pace us in nuclear weapons, and someday be able to destroy us, or worse, blackmail us into subjugation. Better dead than red. By October 1945, just a few weeks after the end of the war against fascism, the United States military was already selecting targets[17] for the war against communism, the last threat to democracy. At the same time, we projected our intentions onto them: that they were hell bent for *our* destruction.

Ever since the end of the Second World War, unbeknownst to the American public, the U. S. military had been planning an all-out assault to destroy the Soviet Union. The intervening decade and a half had not diminished that objective; advances in weapons design and the accumulation of stockpiles had made that objective attainable.

Beginning in 1959 the Strategic Air Command maintained 100 megatons of nuclear weapons flying over the United States, 24 hours a day 7 days a week, 52 weeks a year, to enable a response to a surprise Soviet attack within fifteen minutes.[18] We were living on a nuclear hair-trigger.

The anti-communist fervor also permeated the civilian population. The 1950 revelation by Britain's MI6 that Klaus Fuchs, a prominent scientist from the Manhattan Project, had passed America's atomic secrets to the Russians spawned anticommunist hysteria in the United States. And, where the British sentenced Fuchs to prison, the United States electrocuted his American counterparts, Julius and Ethel Rosenberg. During this period, opportunist Senator Joe McCarthy set off a national witch-hunt when he made bold, but unsubstantiated, claims that there were hundreds of communists in the State Department. He followed these with accusations that communists held positions throughout the Truman Administration, and were even in the United States Army. He never provided any real proof of these allegations, but at the time that did not seem to matter. In the House of Representatives, the Committee on Un-American Activities investigated anyone accused of communist affiliations, or of being what they termed, *fellow travelers*[v]. Hollywood was accused of making pro-communist films. Ten movie executives who invoked their Fifth Amendment rights and refused to answer the committee's questions were imprisoned. Anyone the committee focused on or who refused to name names found themselves blacklisted.

---

[v]   All of this anticommunism did not go un-noticed in the U.S.S.R. The Soviets had some fun in choosing a name for their first satellite. Sputnik is the Russian word for 'fellow traveler.'

In 1958, Eisenhower's National Security Council issued a directive encouraging the military to educate its troops and the public about the dangers of communism, a task they enthusiastically adopted. That same year, Robert Welch, a retired candy maker, founded the John Birch Society as an anti-communist political organization. The group's namesake was an American intelligence officer killed by communists in China in August 1945, who Welch advocated to be the first casualty of the Cold War. However, the group's definition of communism soon became anything that went against their extreme right-wing views. Before long, the military was using the publications of this extremist group as their training material.

~

In 1957, a new Air Force Vice Chief of Staff was sworn in.
It was SAC Commander Curtis E. LeMay, who, as evidenced above:

- Hated communism and wanted all-out war with the soviets;
- Was willing to take matters into his own hands to do it;
- And had become totally numb to the mass slaughter of civilians.

Cuba

On July 26, 1953, a group of about one-hundred-and-forty rebels on the island of Cuba attacked the garrison at Moncada Barracks outside Santiago in a revolt against Dictator Fulgencio Batista. This latest Cuban leader had deposed his predecessor, the freely elected Carlos Prío Socarrás, just the previous year, but already the Batista regime had transformed Cuba into a corrupt and brutal police state.

The rebel attack failed miserably, forcing the survivors to flee into the Sierra Maestra mountains where they were tracked down and captured. The rebel leader, Fidel Castro, was sentenced to fifteen years in prison; however, he was released after serving less than two and made his way to Mexico to plot against Batista anew.

In Mexico Castro met Ernesto "Che" Guevara, an Argentine physician and specialist in guerrilla warfare. Fidel, his brother Raúl, along with Che, and this ragged band of exiles formed the '26th of July Movement,' named after the date of the failed 1953 attack. The rebels turned to KGB contacts in Mexico to obtain much-needed weapons from the Soviet Union. The Russians provided weapons that were untraceable, to avoid drawing the attention of the U.S. The Cubans also scraped together funds from the exile community living in the United States to purchase whatever additional weapons they could. In December 1956, the rebels sailed from Mexico on boats that landed them on Cuban beaches near the city of Manzanillo. Once again, the rebels were quickly routed by Batista's forces and once again, they scattered into the Sierra Maestra Mountains, but this time they evaded capture, and regrouped.

Over the next two years the 26th of July rebels waged a guerrilla campaign against Batista with the assistance and growing support of the Cuban population. In 1957, Castro signed the *Manifesto of the Sierra Maestra* calling for elections within the first 18 months after the defeat of Batista. Stories about these revolutionaries in the New York Times romanticized Castro's rebel cause making him famous in America, and by 1958, the U.S. ceased furnishing arms to Batista. When more and more people joined the rebel movement and the rebels accumulated battlefield victories, the army abandoned the Cuban dictator. On New Year's Day 1959, Batista flew off into exile in the Dominican Republic.

Immediately after their victory Castro pronounced that, "power does not interest me, and I will not take it. From now on the people are entirely free." Rumors spread that he was a communist, but when he visited Washington soon after the revolution, he told a group of Senators, "The 26th of July movement is not a communist movement." However, the entire time Castro was touring the United States, Raúl and Che were making military agreements with the Soviet Union, possibly without his knowledge. But, soon after his return, however, he was sworn in as the Cuban Prime Minister and by the summer of 1959, he had evidently changed his mind about communism, dictators, elections, and power. He moved radically left and discussed plans to communize Cuba. He soon declared that the United States was a "vulture feeding on humanity," renounced standing treaties with the U.S., and dared the Americans to invade. When he began arresting dissidents and suspended habeas corpus, he triggered a new exodus of Cubans to the United States. To strengthen his position in Cuba, he requested and received overt military aid from the Soviet Union and China.

Communism had metastasized onto the Western Hemisphere, only ninety miles from the American mainland. This was a serious problem. Although by 1960 it was too late for Eisenhower to do anything directly, before he left office he initiated a covert plan to remove the new Cuban regime. Presumably, his Vice President, Richard Milhous Nixon, the Republican candidate in the upcoming presidential election, would carry out the invasion plan scheduled for a few months after the inauguration. However, in one of the closest presidential elections in American history, Vice President Nixon was narrowly defeated by the junior senator from Massachusetts, John Fitzgerald Kennedy.

Eisenhower's Farewell Address

Three days before leaving office, 34th President Dwight D. Eisenhower delivered a nationally televised valedictory to the country he had served since youth. Besides the traditional expressions of gratitude and well wishes for the nation, Ike injected an unexpectedly dark warning concerning the military and the industry that supplied it.

> . . . Our military organization today bears little relation to that known by any of my predecessors in peacetime, or, indeed, by the fighting men of World War II or Korea . . . . Until the latest of our world conflicts, the United States had no armaments industry . . . . We have been compelled to create a permanent armaments industry of vast proportions . . . . Now this conjunction of an immense military establishment and a large arms industry is new in the American experience . . . . we must not fail to comprehend its grave implications . . . . The potential for the disastrous rise of misplaced power exists and will persist.

Had this cautionary advice come from a career politician it would have been a warning serious enough. But it was extraordinarily ominous coming from a man who spent his adult life in military service, the former five star general, the iconic hero of World War II, and the man who knew the subject best.

The Case-in-Chief

———•———

merica's 35th President-elect was the second son of Joseph P.
Kennedy, a successful self-made businessman from Boston. The
Kennedy patriarch had worked under Roosevelt when FDR was
secretary of the Navy. In 1938, after JPK's stint as the first chairman
of the Securities and Exchange Commission, Roosevelt appointed him
as ambassador to Great Britain. However, he soon found himself in
hot water with the administration when he expressed strong support
for Chamberlain's Appeasement policies. His support, he said, was an
attempt to prevent another war in Europe, which he believed would
be worse than the first. Without State Department approval, the elder
Kennedy had even sought to meet privately with Hitler to discuss
U.S.-German relations. And later, as the Blitzkrieg rained down on
Britain, he was quoted in a news article saying that democracy was
finished in England, and that it may be in the U.S. as well[19]. Kennedy
was forced to resign in November 1940. His relationship with
Roosevelt was destroyed and the Appeasement stigma was to remain
with him for the rest of his life.

JFK understood the political baggage he inherited from his father's
support of Chamberlain. At Harvard, his senior thesis was a defense
of Chamberlain's appeasement policies. Appeasement was necessary,
he argued, because at the time England and France were not ready
to go to war with Germany, and needed time to re-arm. The thesis
was later published (with plenty of help from the old man) under the
title "*Why England Slept.*" However, it is evident that the younger
Kennedy was very conscious of symbolism; JFK was never seen with
an umbrella, and apparently did not even own one.

In 1941, Jack enlisted in the Navy and served in the Pacific fighting
the Japanese. He earned the Navy and Marine Corps medal when the
Japanese sank his PT boat and his actions saved and later rescued his

crew. After the war, Kennedy mulled over a few career choices, and thought about becoming a journalist or a history professor. But, he decided on politics when the congressional seat in Massachusetts 11th district opened in 1946. He successfully campaigned for the office and served for the next six years. In 1952, he took-on incumbent Henry Cabbot Lodge for one of the state's Senate seats, and won. At the 1956 democratic presidential convention he received national exposure as he graciously accepted defeat after losing the vice presidential nomination to Estes Kefauver of Tennessee. In retrospect, it turned out to be better that he lost that nomination since incumbent President Eisenhower soundly defeated Democratic candidate Adlai Stevenson. JFK was re-elected to the Senate in 1958.

In 1960, he tossed his hat into the presidential race and emerged from a field of democratic primary candidates, survived the Catholic issue, and won the democratic nomination on the first ballot. As his running mate, the young senator, against the advice of his campaign-managing brother Bobby, offered the position to the man he had just defeated for that nomination, Lyndon Johnson of Texas.

During the ensuing campaign, for the first time in American history, the major party candidates conducted live debates on television. The debates between himself and Republican candidate Richard Nixon are credited with giving him just enough of an edge to squeak past the sitting vice president into the White House.

The transition to an incoming administration between the November election and the January inauguration begins with selecting top cabinet posts and making the important appointments. Kennedy began to assemble an administration of intellectuals, who, for the most part were his contemporaries. This provided sharp contrast to the members of the outgoing administration, who were decidedly older. In fact, the oldest serving president to that time was succeeded by the youngest ever elected. As his Secretary of Defense, Kennedy chose Robert McNamara, another Harvard graduate just a year older than himself, who only weeks before had been named the first non-family member to head the Ford Motor Company. However, the new President also tried to establish continuity with the past by asking personnel such as Dean Acheson, Truman's Secretary of State, to become special advisors.

In early January 1961, as an obvious message to the incoming administration, Soviet Premier Nikita Khrushchev delivered a speech proclaiming his nation's support for "wars of national liberation." JFK's inaugural address two weeks later included a response that, amongst other things, pledged to ". . . support any friend, oppose any foe, to assure the survival and the success of liberty." Both men meant exactly what they said. Khrushchev was supporting communist insurgencies in a number of areas of the world; however, soviet soldiers were not involved in direct combat. On close examination of the President's actions, we will find that, while he was prepared to support our friends, this support did not mean having American troops fight in their place. This would quickly become a contentious issue between the President and the Pentagon.

The military of any country can easily remove their leader any time they so choose, as history will attest. The question in this case is motive. Why would America's military decide to turn against this president in 1963? To answer that question, the Prosecution submits as evidence the following synopses of the major relevant events constituting the 1,036 days of the Kennedy administration. The cumulative effect of this review will make their motive apparent.

The first concerned a conflict in a tiny land-locked country in Southeast Asia that few Americans were aware even existed.

Laos–March 1961

When Kennedy took the oath of office, he inherited a conflict that had been festering in Laos, the western neighbor of Vietnam. During the Eisenhower administration, the CIA and the military had deposed the neutral Laotian leader, Souvanna Phouma in favor of anti-communist ruler General Phoumi Nosavan. The Soviet Union, China, and North Vietnam were backing the Pathet Lao communists, and the situation had degenerated into a three-way civil war. Most recently, the communists, with Soviet supplies and logistical support, had taken a strategic area known as the Plain of Jars. On the day before the inauguration, Eisenhower's parting words on the subject were to tell JFK that he might need to intervene in Laos.

Kennedy assigned a task force to the problem that recommended a three-part plan wherein General Phoumi was to recapture the Plain of Jars, the King of Laos would declare neutrality, and the South East Asia Treaty Organization (SEATO) would deploy troops to secure it. The key to the success of this plan was the recapture of the Plain of Jars, which, based on a CIA intelligence estimate, would be an easy task for General Phoumi. That estimate proved to be completely wrong, because when confronted on the battlefield by the Pathet Lao, Phoumi's forces broke and ran. John Kenneth Galbraith, America's Ambassador to India, observed to the President "As a military ally, the entire Laos nation is clearly inferior to a Battalion of conscientious objectors from World War I."

The JCS recommended stepping up U.S. support of Phoumi by sending U.S. combat forces. When Under Secretary of State Chester Bowles argued that the Chinese would not let the introduction of U.S. troops into Laos go unchallenged, the military responded that they had planned for that eventuality. They would simultaneously deploy troops to South Vietnam to block Chinese intervention, and if that was not enough they intended to use nuclear weapons to stop them.

Instead, the President reasoned that Phoumi had demonstrated he was not going to win on his own, and since both our allies and our adversaries preferred the neutral Souvanna, an independent Laos would be better than either abandoning it to the communists, or risk starting World War III with the Chinese. But, communist advances had to be stopped before talks on neutrality could begin, so the task force recommended implementing 'Operation Millpond.' This was a seventeen-step plan of increasing U.S. involvement, the first of which was sending military advisors and the last being massive military intervention. While Kennedy approved the first steps, he specifically withheld approval of the latter. At a news conference on March 23, JFK announced American support for an independent Laos to be determined through an international conference. At the same time, he sent the Seventh Fleet to the South China Sea, ordered 2,500 marines to the Thai border with Laos, and put an additional 10,000 marines in Okinawa on alert as a warning to halt communist advances until the Geneva conference.[20]

American and British calls for that peace conference stalled when the Soviets demanded that the conference begin prior to a cease-fire, rather than the other way around. Meanwhile, the Pathet Lao continued to make gains. Admiral Arleigh Burke, Chief of Naval Operations (CNO), recommended to the President that he issue an ultimatum for a cease-fire, which if unheeded, should be followed by a U.S. attack on the Pathet Lao, and, if necessary, on North Vietnam and Red China too.[21] But, as talks dragged into April, the President's focus shifted to a new crisis.

Operation Zapata–April 1961

The irreparable calamity of the Kennedy administration occurred within its first hundred days. As the 34th President's second term was running out, he directed the military and the CIA to develop covert plans to remove Castro. The initial operation they considered was to overthrow Castro from within by providing supplies and support for anti-Castro guerillas in the Escambray Mountains of Cuba. But this quickly changed because the CIA could not monitor or control this resistance effort and was concerned it could be infiltrated by Castro's agents. The internal uprising plan then morphed into an external amphibious landing of exiles on the beach to be supported by an internal uprising of anti-Castro forces. The CIA formed a brigade of Anti-Castro Cuban exiles, which they were training in Guatemala. President-elect Kennedy was informed of the plan at his Palm Beach home on November 18, 1960.

The plan relied on two critical assumptions:

First, the CIA told the brigade that they were one of several that would be landed on the beaches of Cuba and that they would be backed up by the United States, telling them "if you fail *we* will come in."[22] When planning began under Eisenhower, U.S., intervention was an implicit part of the plan, and likely would have occurred had Richard Nixon won the election. However, the Kennedy administration insisted that this was to be an invasion of Cuba by Cubans, and advised repeatedly, and well in advance, that U.S. military forces were not to be used. In late March, JFK instructed the CIA to tell Brigade leaders that U.S. forces would not be allowed to participate or support invasion in any way, and asked if they thought the invasion would succeed under these conditions. They responded that they still wanted to go ahead, likely disbelieving that last minute disclaimer.

Second, the plan was formed with the erroneous presumption that there was just as much dislike of Castro inside Cuba as there was amongst the exile community, and that an invasion would be supported by an internal uprising. Dislike of Castro may have been rampant among the people who lost money and property in the Cuban revolution and as a result left the island, but Castro had the support of the lower class of Cubans who now felt better off than they did under Batista. Any external invasion supported by the U.S. would be seen as an attempt to restore the former regime. Even those who thought the current leader was bad believed that bringing back the old one would be worse. In addition, two weeks before leaving the White House, the Eisenhower administration cut diplomatic relations with Cuba. This also cut off communication with agents inside Cuba for any expected revolt. Only very late in the planning did Admiral Burke advise the President that the success of the entire operation was contingent upon a general uprising.

The President tried to "reduce the noise" of the operation by changing the landing site from Trinidad beach to a site on the Zapata peninsula called the 'Bahía de Cochinos,' or, in English 'The Bay of Pigs', the name for which this operation would forever-after be identified. This landing site was more remote from major population centers and, with a night landing, would be less conspicuous. In addition, the President ordered that the number of planes attacking the Cuban airfields be reduced from sixteen to eight. CIA Deputy Director of Plans, Richard Bissell, accepted these changes without telling the President the adverse effects that he knew these decisions would have on the invasion's outcome. JFK considered stopping the plan entirely, but after having made an issue of Eisenhower's lack of action on Cuba during the campaign, it would have been difficult to cancel it now that he was in office.

Kennedy also sought out independent opinions from other sources in his administration. "Are you serious?" advisor Dean Acheson asked incredulously when the President sounded him out about the plan, "It doesn't take Price Waterhouse to tell you that 1,500 Cubans (invaders) are not as good as 25,000 Cubans (Castro's soldiers)."[23] But legendary CIA Director Allen Dulles told Kennedy that the plan had a higher chance of success than the 1954 coup that the CIA conducted against Jacobo Árbenz in Guatemala under Eisenhower. And the Joint Chiefs assured the President that the Cuban air force was disorganized, having only obsolete and inoperative equipment, and that Cuban forces would largely desert Castro when the invasion began. In addition, there was a backup plan that if all else failed the invaders could follow Castro's script and escape into the mountains to fight a guerilla campaign. With these firm assurances from the CIA and the Joint Chiefs, Kennedy reluctantly gave the go-ahead.

What Dulles did not reveal about the Árbenz coup was that it had nearly been a complete disaster, because when the time came to fight, the CIA trained rebels refused. Only by an incredible stroke of dumb luck, the Guatemalan forces turned out to be even less inclined to fight, and because they were so terrified that the U.S. was about to invade, they instead forced Árbenz to resign.[24]

Any thought about the element of surprise had to be abandoned since it was common knowledge in Cuba that an invasion was coming, as revealed in articles in the American press about exiles training in Guatemala. "Castro doesn't need any agents over here; all he has to do is read our papers." JFK wryly observed.[25]

On April 15 the planned air strikes from Nicaragua were launched against Castro's air force using un-marked B-26's flown by Cuban pilots. But timing of the strike was botched because the pilots arrived late, after they neglected to take the difference in time zone into account, [26]and as a result proved ineffective as they destroyed only five planes. A planned second air strike, intended to cover the landing, was cancelled by the President, because it could not be credibly claimed to be launched from the Brigade on the beachhead. Castro's remaining air force proved much better than advertised and instead of abandoning him; they attacked invaders throughout the operation. In a fantastically bad piece of planning, all of the Brigade's ammunition, along with most of their communication equipment was lost during the landing when the single ship they were loaded on was sunk by Castro's planes. Once on the beach, the rebels found the escape route impassible due to the eight miles of swamp between the landing site and the Escambray Mountains. And any hope of an internal uprising disappeared when Castro rounded up and arrested anyone suspected of having connections to Cuban resistance groups.

Approximately one-hundred-thousand people were taken into custody and herded into auditoriums and theaters.

In Washington, the situation came to a head in a meeting convened in the Cabinet Room on the evening of April 18, with the President and the Joint Chiefs attending in formal dress after just coming from a reception for Congress in the White House. The Joint Chiefs and the CIA recommended providing assistance with naval forces they had stationed just off the Cuban coast, contrary to the President's prior orders. After a discussion lasting several hours, Kennedy refused to intervene. In the end, the outnumbered Brigade, surrounded by Castro's forces, surrendered on April 20.

Blame and recrimination for the disaster began immediately. JFK angrily blamed the CIA and the Joint Chiefs for lying to him about the plan. In the aftermath of the fiasco, JFK discovered that the JCS and the CIA had known all along that the invasion would never work without American help and had counted on maneuvering him into a position where he would be forced to approve U.S. intervention. Furthermore, Dulles and Bissell knew this as far back as the previous November when they first briefed JFK in Palm Springs. Kennedy subsequently threatened to "splinter the CIA into a thousand pieces and scatter it to the winds." In the ensuing weeks, the President issued three orders under National Security Action Memorandums (NSAM), numbers NSAM 55, NSAM 56, and NSAM 57. These orders took responsibility for covert operations such as this away from the CIA and assigned them to the Joint Chiefs of Staff. Henceforth the JCS were to develop, review and concur with any paramilitary operations before recommending them to the president.

Conversely, CIA Director Dulles and Deputy Director of Plans Bissell placed the blame on JFK because he cancelled the second air strike. An article in the September 1961 issue of Fortune magazine by Washington Bureau Chief Charles Murphy, gave an account of the Bay of Pigs that blamed the President. JFK was convinced that General Charles Cabal was the source of leak; however, years later Murphy revealed that Admiral Burke was the actual source of the information. The Admiral felt that JFK had "chickened out" in not calling for naval air support for the invasion. According to Murphy, Burke had nothing but contempt for President Kennedy. [27]

> At an April 21 breakfast meeting attended by Rusk, McGeorge Bundy, and others, Kennedy, who had been reading stories in the paper about who was to blame for the Bay of Pigs, commented "acidly" that the Chiefs were not mentioned, which meant that the stories had been leaked by the Pentagon.[28]

In the aftermath of the Bay of Pigs failure, there were calls from the right for Kennedy's impeachment. In off-the-record remarks made during an interview with a columnist for the Washington Post, LeMay accused President Kennedy of outright cowardice for his decision to not use U.S. forces in the Bay of Pigs operation. LeMay spoke to some of his staff about the 'theoretical' removal of a president from office. The overall temperament of the interview gave the reporter, Fletcher Knebel, the idea for a story about a military overthrow of the U.S. government. It resulted in the book *Seven Days in May*, which he co-authored with Charles W. Bailey 2nd. After reading the novel, Kennedy, in discussing the plot with friends, mused that,

> It's possible. It could happen in this country, but the conditions would have to be just right. If, for example, the country had a young president, and he had a Bay of Pigs, there would be certain uneasiness. Maybe the military would do a little criticizing behind his back, but this would be written off as the usual military dissatisfaction with civilian control. Then if there were another Bay of Pigs, the reaction of the country would be, 'Is he too young and inexperienced?' The military would almost feel that it was their patriotic obligation to stand ready to preserve the integrity of the nation, and only God knows just what segment of democracy they would be defending if they overthrew the elected establishment . . . . Then, if there were a third Bay of Pigs, it could happen.[29]

President Kennedy encouraged Director John Frankenheimer to film Seven Days in May "as a warning to the republic.[30]

Laos—April 1961

Only days after the Cuban debacle, the problem in Laos was back. Moscow had finally agreed to a cease-fire, but the Pathet Lao were bent on seizing as much territory as they could until it took effect. Phoumi pleaded for American airstrikes to fend them off. Admiral Burke, anticipating that orders for intervention would soon be issued, ordered Naval assets in the Pacific to prepare to attack Laos, North Vietnam and bases in China.

At a meeting between the President and the Joint Chiefs, Burke sat in for Chairman Lemnitzer, who was in Laos evaluating the situation first hand. The Admiral argued strongly that SEATO troops should be deployed immediately, in addition to as many U.S. troops as could be sent at once. When JFK asked if sending the requested troops would deplete our reserve or affect our ability to respond to a Soviet move in Berlin, Burke admitted that it would. A chaotic argument amongst the chiefs then ensued as to the logistics of sending large numbers of soldiers. In the end, the Chiefs concluded that the U.S. had to intervene, but that because not enough troops could get there in time, the President would probably also need to use nuclear weapons.

Seeking congressional opinions, JFK opened the meeting to include a number of House and Senate leaders. This wider audience heard the same argument from Burke; that the United States needed to intervene in Laos, even if in meant nuclear war, because if we do not fight here, then we would have to fight in Thailand or Vietnam, and where would we draw the line? Despite this impassioned plea, the almost-unanimous consensus was that we should not intervene in Laos. The only exception was Vice President Lyndon Johnson, who whole-heartedly agreed with Burke. [31] At Johnson's request, the Joint Chiefs were allowed two days to coordinate and clarify their recommendations.

By the follow-up meeting, they now unanimously recommended intervention. McNamara, Burke, and Army General Decker thought that the Chinese would attack if the U.S. intervened, so we would need to use nuclear weapons. While LeMay, Rusk and Bohlen believed the Chinese would not step in, but LeMay thought it would be just as well if they did, because he beleived it was "high time we get to work on China" anyway. But the Chiefs were not any more prepared for the President's most basic questions. They had no answer when he asked what they had planned in case the communists attacked before we had all of our forces landed on the limited Laotian airfields.

> The President was appalled at the sketchy nature of the American military planning for Laos—the lack of detail and the unanswered questions. [32]

He was not alone in this thinking, his Special Advisor Dean Acheson

> . . . thought that these Chiefs "not nearly as good" as those serving during Truman's administration. "In fact I am shocked—and I think the Secretary of Defense is also, at the shoddy work that comes out of the military . . . . For what we spend on them we deserve something better than we get." [33]

The President turned to Douglas McArthur who told him that anyone who proposed sending U.S. combat forces into Asia should have his head examined. A jungle war, he said, would suit the communists. The President decided against American intervention.

Meanwhile, Lemnitzer continued to recommend sending in U.S. forces and publically criticized the neutral Laos plan.[34] The Laotian crisis peaked less than a week after the Bay of Pigs fiasco, in which none of the Chiefs assurances or predictions turned out to be true. Kennedy's view of the military advice he was receiving had changed dramatically. He remarked to Arthur Schlesinger that

"If it hadn't been for Cuba, we might be about to intervene in Laos." Waving a sheaf of cables from Lemnitzer, he added, "I might have taken this advice seriously."[35]

Because of his refusal to intervene militarily and because he was willing to negotiate with the Russians, Kennedy was accused of appeasement in Laos.[36]

Vienna–June 1961

Back in February, Kennedy proposed a face-to-face meeting to Soviet Premier Khrushchev for June of that year. But with no response by April and in the aftermath of the Bay of Pigs, Kennedy presumed the meeting was a dead issue. Khrushchev, however, unexpectedly accepted the invitation in mid-May, and both agreed that the agenda would include Laos, a Test Ban Treaty, and Berlin.

On Laos, Kennedy and Khrushchev acknowledged that neither was interested in a war in the jungles, and agreed on a neutral Laos. At this point, it was easy for Khrushchev to agree to theoretical neutrality since the communists held the upper hand there. However, this was to be the only progress made at the two-day meeting.

On other issues Khrushchev went on the offensive, lecturing the much younger president about the merits of communism, arguing that it was the wave of the future, and that American intervention in Cuba had been an attempt to interfere with the right of people to throw off imperialism. Khrushchev obviously relished the opportunity to rub Kennedy's nose in the failed invasion attempt. Kennedy countered that, while he would not defend the Batista regime, and agreed with people's right to free themselves from oppression, in the Cuban case, after their revolution succeeded; a minority of communists had taken control over the country against the will of the people. Furthermore, he pointed out, the Russians were in no position to lecture the U.S. after the Soviet invasion of Hungary in 1956 to crush their anti-communist uprising.

Atmospheric testing of atomic weapons was a serious concern in the early 1960's. Since World War II, first the U.S., and then the Russians, were conducting scores of aboveground nuclear weapon test explosions, with the ensuing radioactive dust dispersing in the upper elevations of the atmosphere and spreading worldwide[37]. Khrushchev argued against a test ban treaty on the grounds that the requisite number inspections were an American attempt at espionage. Furthermore, the Soviets would consider a test ban treaty only if it was tied to total disarmament. The U.S. would not agree to total disarmament, as it only benefitted the Soviets, since it would automatically put them on even parity. However, Khrushchev said he would continue discussions in Geneva, as well as extend the moratorium on aboveground testing, as long as the U.S. did likewise.

The most contentious issue on the agenda was Berlin. Khrushchev stated that it had been sixteen years since the end of the war and that for the Soviets the existing situation was intolerable. As Khrushchev once said to a U.S. diplomat, "it would be like having a piece of the Soviet Union in Iowa; you would not accept it." Berlin had become an acute problem for Khrushchev because every year hundreds of thousands of people were escaping from the communist sector into West Berlin, particularly those with educations, and he had to stop the exodus. He warned JFK that Russia would sign a separate peace treaty with East Germany allowing it to take over all of Berlin. Any attempt by the west to access West Berlin thereafter would be an act of aggression against a sovereign East Germany, the consequence of which would be war. Then, revealing his awareness of American military intentions, Khrushchev remarked mockingly:

> Maybe we should sign an agreement right away and get
> it over with, *that is what the Pentagon had wanted.*
> [Emphasis added]

Kennedy argued that the U.S. had won the right to be in Berlin, and would not be forced out; it was the Soviets who wanted to change the status quo. Concluding the long discussion, Khrushchev warned that he would sign an agreement in December, and if the U.S. wanted war that was their problem, and if so, the Soviets would accept the challenge. Kennedy responded, "Then, Mr. Chairman, there will be war. It will be a cold winter."

The President came away disturbed at the intransigence of the Soviet leader and mystified by his apparent indifference to the horror of nuclear war. Although JFK held his ground and countered the Soviet Premier on every point, the President's reasonable tone and

49

intellectual style contrasted sharply with the bellicose bombast of his Soviet counterpart, leaving the distinct impression that Khrushchev had pushed around a weaker Kennedy.

U.S. analysts had concluded that the liquid-fueled Jupiter missiles promised to Italy and Turkey by Eisenhower were technologically obsolete. Kennedy considered pursuing other options instead, such as positioning American submarines armed with newly developed and more reliable solid-fueled Polaris missiles in the Mediterranean. But, in light of JFK's Vienna meeting with Khrushchev, rescinding Eisenhower's missile deal just then would look particularly weak, and the suggestion was not received well by either receiving NATO ally[38].

The Berlin Crisis—Summer 1961

A few days after their Vienna meeting, Khrushchev announced on Soviet TV that the U.S.S.R. would sign a peace treaty with East Germany by the end of the year. Shortly thereafter, the Soviets also dropped all pretense of serious negotiation of a test ban treaty in Geneva. Throughout the rest of June and July, the communists escalated the crisis, as East German President Walter Ulbricht threatened to close off access to West Berlin, and let it be known that this time, the blockade would include the airport.

Near the end of June, Dean Acheson finished the report that the President requested him to prepare enumerating U.S. options in Berlin. Acheson's paper advised taking a hard line, even if it meant all-out war. His assumption was that Khrushchev was only provoking a crisis to test America's will to resist, and that if he could force us to back down from our commitment to West Berlin, he could destroy our prestige and credibility worldwide.

Acheson recommended that if the threatened treaty was signed and our access to West Berlin was denied, we must respond immediately. Our first step should be with an airlift, and if they interfered then we must act militarily. He further recommended that the President immediately initiate a military buildup in West Berlin. Acheson believed that the military buildup itself may demonstrate to Khrushchev the west's commitment to fight and convince him to back off; but if not, we must be prepared for thermonuclear war.

In early July, the Pentagon leaked U.S. contingency plans for evacuation of non-essential personnel from West Berlin along with the possible deployment of nuclear weapons to advance ready positions. According to an article appearing in the July 19 Washington Post, LeMay told guests at a recent Georgetown dinner party that a nuclear war would breakout later that year and that major cities such as Washington, New York, Philadelphia, Los Angeles, Chicago and Detroit would be destroyed.

Khrushchev believed, and the West Germans suspected, that JFK would surrender West Berlin rather than go to war. A story appeared in the American press, most likely another leak from the Pentagon, that Soviet Ambassador Mikhail Menshikov had advised Khrushchev that "Kennedy didn't amount to much; didn't have much courage." In the two months since Khrushchev's treaty announcement, the President seemed to be avoiding the issue, as he made no public statement regarding the escalating series of threats.

And at this early point in his presidency, as the superpowers approached what he described during the campaign would be a time of "maximum danger" in the 1960's, he showed that he was determined to exhaust every possible alternative to avoid war, including negotiations. Or, at the least in this case, going through the motions of negotiations. Yet, despite his urging, the State Department was unable to develop a negotiating strategy, because in reality, the West had nothing to negotiate. Of all countries involved in Berlin, it was only the Soviets who wanted to alter the existing arrangements. JFK clearly understood this, as he told Finland's president "The Soviet Union is asking for concessions in exchange for which they will give us what we already have. We would be buying the same horse twice." Finally, if only as a symbolic gesture, the President had Acheson suggest a Foreign Ministers conference amongst the western powers. These would be in preparation for talks with the Soviets sometime after West German elections in September. However, the negotiating position remained maintaining the status quo.

But, the mere suggestion of negotiation was anathema to our allies and to the U.S. military. The Republican National Chairman stated that the Kennedy Administration's attitude in general is one of appeasement toward Communism throughout the world. At a news conference, he was asked if

> . . . members of your Administration . . . have felt that sharp Republican warnings against appeasement have constricted the room that you may have to negotiate with the Russians?

To which the President responded:

> No. I am going to attempt, as I have said, to protect our vital
> interests, and see whether it is possible for us to reach an
> agreement in this matter, which will not necessitate a war,
> which could mean so much destruction for so many millions
> and millions of people in this country and elsewhere.[39]

On July 25, Kennedy responded to the growing crisis with a televised address to the nation. He announced a number of measures that the government was taking, including a military buildup in Germany, increased defense spending, building additional fallout shelters, and calling up reservists. Although the actions were for the most part military, he stated that the West still hoped for a peaceful resolution of the crisis, summarizing, "we seek peace, but we shall not surrender." The Soviet Premier interpreted Kennedy's actions as an ultimatum, and on August 7 announced that reciprocal measures were being taken by the U.S.S.R.

In the press, Richard Nixon called the movement of American troops into West Berlin a useless gesture that Khrushchev might interpret as weakness rather than strength. When asked about Nixon's comment at the next news conference, the President responded rhetorically, "If troops were withdrawn, would that strengthen it?"[40]

Meanwhile, refugees by the thousands continued to pour across the border into West Berlin, resulting in imposition of even heavier travel restrictions. Then, just after midnight on August 13, thousands of East German troops appeared at all border crossings and began erecting barricades and barbed wire. A few days later, construction of the more permanent concrete Berlin Wall began, completely closing West Berlin from East Germany. So much for communism as the wave of the future. Expressing their displeasure at Kennedy's refusal to take any action against erection of the wall, students at the University of Berlin sent the President a LARGE BLACK UMBRELLA.[41]

But, to boost German confidence in U.S. resolve and to demonstrate our continued access to Berlin, Kennedy sent Vice President

Johnson[42] and retired General Lucius Clay, the architect of the 1948 airlift, to Berlin on August 17. JFK thought their presence in West Berlin would send the right message to both the Germans and the Soviets, so the Vice President and the General were there to meet the 1,500 U.S. soldiers who had made the 110-mile trip down the autobahn through East Germany without incident. Contrary to his personal assurances to Kennedy in Vienna, Khrushchev responded with an enormous aboveground nuclear test. Clearly carried out as psychological intimidation, the fifty-megaton explosion remains to this day the largest thermonuclear device ever detonated by mankind.

But then, once the bleeding of refugees to the west had been stopped, Khrushchev seemed to look for a pretext to end the crisis. He told famous Washington columnist, Drew Pearson, who was visiting the Soviet Union at the time, that there was not going to be a war. A back channel communication was established through Mikhail Karmalov, the Soviet Press spokesman, who on September 24th delivered a message to White House Press Secretary Pierre Salinger. Khrushchev's message was that he hoped the President's address to the United Nations the next day would not be an ultimatum like the one of July 25. Kennedy's U.N. speech, while placing blame for the crisis squarely on the Kremlin, expressed the President's belief that a peaceful solution to the crisis was possible, as long as there was freedom in Berlin. Three days after the U.N. speech, Khrushchev sent Kennedy a twenty-six page conciliatory letter, via the Karmalov-Salinger link, seeking a peaceful solution to Berlin. A few weeks later, Khrushchev announced to the 22nd Congress of the Soviet Communist Party that the West had shown some understanding of the situation and were inclined to seek a solution to the Berlin problem, so a separate treaty did not need to be signed. The immediate crisis was over.

However, the problem was left unresolved and tensions on the ground remained high. At the end of October, East German Police began to harass western diplomats' access to East Berlin. After one such incident, General Clay took it upon himself to respond with a demonstration of allied resolve and lined up American tanks at a border crossing known as 'Checkpoint Charlie.' The Russians responded in kind, and before long dozens of Soviet and American tanks faced-off a few meters across the borderline, all of them with live ordinance aimed directly at one another, and both sides had orders to fire-if-fired-upon. All-out war would have broken out if either had so much as flinched. NATO and SAC went on alert. The tense standoff continued for sixteen hours until it was finally resolved by the President via the recently established back channel to the Soviet Premier. Kennedy relayed the message to Khrushchev that American tanks would withdraw if Soviet tanks did so first. Kennedy personally telephoned Clay and told him that when the Soviet tanks backed away to "get those goddamned tanks out of sight." Khrushchev gave the order, and as each Russian tank backed away, an American tank reciprocated.

Afterward, the commander of the U.S. Army in Europe, General Bruce Clarke, questioned Clay's conduct during this incident. There were reports that in the weeks prior to the standoff, Clay had workers build concrete replicas of the Berlin Wall in the nearby woods, and that our tanks had been seen demolishing them.[43] Notably, in the photographs taken during the standoff, the American tanks that faced the Russians at Checkpoint Charlie have bulldozer plows affixed to their front ends.

On February 25, 2010, the Defense Department denied a Freedom of Information Act (FOIA) request for documents related to contingency plans from the 1961 Berlin Crisis. These still need to remain secret, according to the Pentagon, "for fear of damage to current U.S. national security." Seriously? What could possibly be concealed in fifty-year-old documents regarding a city that is no longer divided, and a confrontation with a country that no longer exists, that could be a threat to the security of the United States in 2010? What could the military possibly have been planning that they still cannot reveal, five decades after the crisis ended? Had the military been planning to take matters into their own hands and destroy the Berlin Wall in order to force a confrontation with the Soviets?

The Net Evaluation Subcommittee—July 1961

During the Berlin Crisis, the President requested a review and critique of the Acheson Report from his special assistant, Arthur Schlesinger. Included in Schlesinger's response was the recommendation that if the Pentagon really believed that war was our only option, they should advise the President as to what the actual consequences of such an outcome would be.

> The paper hinges on our willingness to face nuclear war. But this option is undefined. Before you are asked to make the decision to go to nuclear war, you are entitled to know what concretely nuclear war is likely to mean. The Pentagon should be required to make an analysis of the possible levels and implications of nuclear warfare and the possible gradations of our own nuclear response.[44]

Two weeks later, on July 20, a meeting of the National Security Council was held at which the *Net Evaluation Subcommittee* presented the requested analysis. The only reason we know anything about this meeting is because Vice President Johnson was unable to attend, so he sent his military aide, Air Force Colonel Howard Burris, in his place. Afterward, the Colonel sent Johnson his notes of that presentation, which were declassified in 1993, and have since become known as the *Burris Memorandum*.[45] These notes show that the military had confirmed that the US was far ahead in nuclear capability and that there was a window of opportunity where the U.S. could launch a pre-emptive strike against the Soviet Union and prevail. They recommended to the President that the strike be launched in the form of:

> . . . a surprise attack in late 1963, preceded by a period of heightened tensions . . . .

> The President posed the question as to the period of time necessary for citizens to remain in shelters following an

attack. A member of the Subcommittee replied that no specific period of time could be cited due to the variables involved, but generally speaking, a period of two weeks should be expected.[46]

The President directed that no member in attendance at the meeting disclose even the subject of the meeting.

JFK walked out of the room in disgust, commenting, "And we call ourselves the human race."

Eisenhower had rejected the pre-emptive attack plan in 1953 with the military clout that the former five-star general possessed. But with the beginnings of satellite information and the intervening American weapons buildup, the military had verification of just how far ahead the U.S. actually was, and were seriously reconsidering the plan. While the generals may have respected Eisenhower, they had slight regard for his replacement, whose military service Lemnitzer denigrated as "some sort of patrol boat skipper." As Eisenhower himself remarked in his final days as president, "God help any man who sits behind this desk who doesn't know the military like I do."

SIOP-62 Briefing–September 1961

On September 13, 1961, another meeting was held between the military, President Kennedy, and his advisors. This was a more in depth presentation of military planning and strategy for nuclear war, which also included responses to a number of the questions on this subject raised by JFK during the July meeting.

Prior to 1960, Commanders-In-Chief of the various U.S. military commands prepared their own plans for the use of nuclear weapons. This resulted in duplication of some targets while neglecting others. In late 1960, Eisenhower's Defense Department established a new organization called the *Joint Strategic Target Planning Staff (JSTPS)* to develop a coordinated nuclear war plan. The plan produced by the JSTPS was entitled the *Single Integrated Operating Plan* or *SIOP*. The first version of the plan was *SIOP-62*, which was approved by the JCS in December 1960 and became effective the following April, after Eisenhower had left office.

General Lemnitzer, JCS Chairman, presented the plan, enumerating the various military and urban-industrial targets in the Soviet Union and China, referred to as one target, the *Sino-Soviet bloc*. He identified specifics on the number of warheads and their effects in such a condescending fashion that Kennedy later remarked was "as though we were kindergartners."

The briefing did, however, make clear a number of items. It was true that American possessed a significant advantage in the total number of nuclear weapons. But in addition, because of the pre-emptive attack planning and the Gaither Report recommendations implemented by Eisenhower, the U.S. was significantly more prepared than they to launch a nuclear strike. Half of SAC bombers were on fifteen-minute ready alert, with additional bombers already airborne. Two Polaris submarines, each with sixteen missiles, were also on alert, as were twenty-four of SAC's seventy-eight ICBMs.

This contrasted sharply with the U.S.S.R., which had none of their ICBMs on alert, with their warheads stored separately and controlled by the KGB. The liquid fuel for their ICBMs would take several hours to load onto the rockets. No Soviet bombers were on runway alert and none were airborne, and many of their submarines were in port.

Because their ramp-up time was much longer than ours, any signal that they were preparing a nuclear attack, such as attaching warheads to ICBMs, fueling missiles, loading and dispersing bombers, would allow enough time for the U.S. to pre-empt it. However, the military advised that any pre-emptive attack could never be one hundred percent effective. Under any scenario, some portion of the Soviet weapons would be delivered to their targets in the U.S. with significant American casualties.

Although the SIOP was efficient, it was rigid and inflexible. There were no options to adjust our response to deal with the specific conditions of an emerging conflict. It consisted of a single convulsive all-out attack using our entire arsenal, launched against targets in the *Sino-Soviet bloc*, whether both were involved in the conflict or not. The military's main reasoning for this was that, if we launched only a portion of our weapons, the enemy may destroy those kept in reserve, plus U.S. casualties would increase if we held back and allowed the communists to counterattack.[47]

The Kennedy administration's reaction to this rigid plan was extremely negative. The President ordered major changes to the plan to incorporate more options, along with a flexible target mix.

The military maintained that the U.S. could prevail in such a war. Clearly, the military and the President had a completely different understanding of what 'prevailing' meant. General Thomas Power, LeMay's successor as commander of SAC, stated that as long as "there were two Americans left and only one Russian, we win!" Conversely, the President believed that "only fools could cling to the idea of victory in a nuclear war."

Vietnam–November 1961

Over the previous millennium, the nation we now know as Vietnam had been in an almost continuous struggle to either maintain, or regain its independence from China. In 1885 the French assisted settling a civil war there, but afterward insinuated themselves into a gradual takeover of the region. For the next fifty-five years, the country became incorporated into the colonial empire known as French Indochina, which also included modern-day Cambodia, and Laos.

During World War II, with their army crushed by the Wehrmacht, the French started a resistance movement to help regain their independence. At the same time, forces for the independence of Vietnam, known as the Viet Minh, were assisting the Allies in their fight against the Japanese. With the end of the war within reach, President Roosevelt privately made it clear to the French that when the war was over they would not be allowed to re-claim their old colonies.

On September 2, 1945, as Douglas MacArthur was receiving the Japanese surrender aboard the USS Missouri, communist leader Ho Chi Minh was in Hanoi proclaiming independence for the Democratic Republic of Vietnam. However, by then, the French had been liberated from the Germans, and Roosevelt was dead. The French promptly sent in forces to re-assert control. And, in keeping with America's new "CONTAINMENT" policy, French actions had the support of Roosevelt's successor. The Viet Minh began a guerilla war to resist French re-colonization.

In 1951, as that war intensified, the Representative from Massachusetts's 11th Congressional District, being keenly interested in foreign affairs, took his sister Pat and his younger brother Bobby on a seven-week 25,000 mile tour to educate himself on the effectiveness of American policies around the world. On the way, he met with foreign political and military leaders, businessmen, and private citizens of numerous countries in the near, Middle and Far East. On his return, Congressman John Kennedy gave an account of what he learned. In regards to Southeast Asia, he had this to report:

> In Indochina, we have allied ourselves to the desperate effort of a French regime to hang on to the remnants of empire. There is no broad, general support of the native Vietnam government among the people of that area. To check the southern drive of communism makes sense, but not only through reliance on the force of arms. The task is rather to build strong native non-Communist sentiment within these areas and rely on that as a spearhead of defense rather than upon the legions of General de Lattre, brilliant though they may be. To do this apart from and in defiance of innately nationalistic aims spells foredoomed failure.

His assessment was correct; the French were slowly but surely losing. By Spring 1954, the Viet Minh army cornered the French garrison in a fort at Dien Bien Phu, where, after a fifty-seven day siege, the French surrendered. Following their defeat, a peace conference in Geneva produced a set of agreements intended to settle the conflict. These accords separated Vietnam into a northern zone led by Ho Chi Minh, and a southern State of Vietnam, headed by former Emperor Bao Dai. The final declaration of the Conference stipulated that Vietnam would be reunified through general elections to be held no later than July 1956. However, delegates of South Vietnam and the United States refused to accept this final declaration.

To prevent the Asian nation from falling to the communists, Eisenhower sent military advisors to prop-up the South Vietnamese regime. A key member of that mission was Colonel Edward Geary Lansdale, an expert in psychological warfare, special operations, and military intelligence. In World War II, he joined the OSS, the predecessor of the CIA, and later served as an instructor at the Strategic Intelligence School in Colorado. He was selected for the Vietnam assignment because of his successful defeat of a communist insurgency in the Philippines after World War II. In Vietnam Lansdale set up a covert network to take out the communist infrastructure left over from the fight against the French. In 1955, he helped South Vietnam' s Prime Minister, Ngo Dinh Diem, maneuver a takeover of the government through a rigged referendum. Diem quickly proclaimed himself president of the Republic of Vietnam, and with U.S. encouragement, balked at holding the elections prescribed by the Geneva accords because there was no doubt he would lose. A new guerilla war began, and pro-Hanoi Viet Cong, infiltrating from the north through Laos, began to attack southern villages.

During this period, Lansdale had to help Diem survive a number of attempted military coups. The problem with Diem was that he did not have widespread support; he was repressive, aloof, and remote from the people. The fact that he was Roman Catholic magnified his disconnection with them because Catholicism was brought in by the French, where the Vietnamese were predominately Buddhists. His religion identified him with colonial rule, something that the Viet Cong frequently used for propaganda advantage. After Diem survived another attempted coup in 1960, he turned even more repressive, and began to pit his generals against each other to prevent their scheming against him. He brutally crushed any and all opposition, accusing anyone who disagreed with him of being a communist.

Once the Joint Chiefs realized that JFK was not going to send troops to Laos, they shifted their focus towards sending them to South Vietnam. They put their recommendations into a memo to the President in May suggesting that President Diem be encouraged to request U.S. troops as part of our SEATO agreement. This memo was issued just as JFK planned to send the Vice President to South Vietnam to reassure Diem in the wake of the Laos decision. On his arrival in Vietnam, LBJ received a Top Secret cable from the JCS, which they sent through the military station in Saigon so that no one from the State Department would see it. It was a transcript of their troop recommendation to the President. On the trip, Johnson superficially followed the President's instructions, but then went far beyond them. He promised Diem that the US would fund his requested 20,000-man increase to his army. Plus Diem's new request, made to LBJ at this meeting, for an additional 100,000-man increase would be accepted if he also asked for 16,000 U. S. combat troops as "direct training personnel." This is precisely what the JCS memo suggested. The Joint Chiefs had bypassed the President by having Johnson take their troop recommendation to Diem. But the President got wind of their scheme and, through back channels, let it be known to the Vietnamese that even before the requests were made, they would be denied.

All through that summer and into the fall, as the Kennedy administration focus was drawn to the crisis in Berlin, communist infiltration and attacks in South Vietnam increased significantly. And more often than not, when confronted, Diem's forces would flee into the jungle. In early October, Diem made an official request for American combat troops through Ambassador Nolting. The President decided to send Maxwell Taylor to assess the situation, saying he would base his decision on the retired General's recommendation. With Taylor's reputation for being an intellectual and an original thinker, Kennedy expected an answer that would better address the insurgency, as opposed to the insistence for conventional military intervention he was getting from the JCS. But, to JFK's great dissatisfaction, Taylor came back with a plan for exactly what he did not want. The General proposed that the U.S. commit its combat troops, but under the guise of humanitarian relief for recent flooding in the Mekong delta.

The majority of his advisors, including McNamara, now strenuously urged American intervention. However, the President was dead set against it, in no small part because none of those advisors could answer his primary question: why were the Viet Cong winning? To JFK there was something fundamentally wrong if Diem could not defeat a relatively few insurgents with a large standing army. Moreover, he believed that conventional warfare was an inappropriate response to the nature of the problem. "Sending in troops," he said, "would be like taking a drink; the effect wears off. We'll have to send in more and more. If this turned into a white man's war then we would lose the way the French did in 1954."

The President issued his decision in NSAM 111 on November 22, 1961. While he did agree to send significantly more equipment and

4

advisors, he would not authorize combat troops for South Vietnam. He never wavered from that policy for the two years he had left to live.

Later that week, Kennedy made major changes to the personnel in his administration. Known as the 'Thanksgiving Day Massacre,' those who disagreed with his policies in Southeast Asia found themselves replaced with others who did. As part of this shake up, he also fired CIA chief Allen Dulles and his deputy, Charles Cabell for the Bay of Pigs.

The Right—1961

In the early 1960's a number of radical right wing groups were on the rise. Historian Arthur Schlesinger tells us that these groups become most extreme whenever a progressive president comes into office. This was certainly the case in the early 30's when groups like this were convinced that Roosevelt was turning the country into a socialist state. After the election of John F. Kennedy, the number and vitriol of these groups rose sharply. The two most strident were the *John Birch Society* and the *Minutemen*. They shared a rabid hatred of communism, the United Nations, and Supreme Court Justice Earl Warren. And they were becoming increasingly shrill. The founder of the John Birch Society had even labeled Eisenhower as a "conscious agent of the communist conspiracy."

The newer, more militant group was the *Minutemen*. The group was founded in 1961 by Robert DePugh who feared an imminent communist takeover of the U.S. They organized into cells around the country and stockpiled weapons in preparation for the coming fight against "subversives." These groups felt it was their patriotic duty to rise up to save the country because of the new administration's weakness.

Three days after the inauguration, as the new administration was just moving in, Admiral Burke submitted the text of an upcoming speech to Defense Secretary Robert McNamara's office. The speech included a virulent attack of the Soviet Union. In those early days, the President was in the midst of negotiating an offer from Khrushchev to free two American fliers who had been shot down the previous July on one of LeMay's spy missions. The U.S., of course, claimed the plane was over international waters. After reviewing the Admiral's speech, the President's staff returned it with instructions to turn down the rhetoric. Subsequently, the President ordered that all speeches by active duty officers were to receive prior review by the White House. Burke made the required changes, but he also passed the story on to the press. A furor soon arose, which would later lead to hearings in the Senate Armed Services Committee that the administration was "muzzling the military." However, the small detail that Burke omitted when he leaked the story was that his speeches had been subject to the exact same scrutiny and revision countless times before under Eisenhower. In fact, he submitted this latest one to the Defense Secretary without being asked. The not so subtle message was that JFK must be soft on communism since he would not let Burke say anything negative about the Soviet Union.

Major General Edwin Walker was commander of the 24th infantry division in West Germany when he instituted mandatory anti-communist training and distributed right wing literature to his troops, including publications from the *John Birch Society*. He also began taking political stands, instructing his soldiers how they should vote, and all of his recommendations were for conservative Republicans. All of this was clearly against regulations, for which he had previously been criticized by President Eisenhower. But, after he was quoted by a newspaper as saying that Harry Truman, Eleanor Roosevelt, and Dean Acheson were "definitely pink," he was relieved of command. Rather than accept re-assignment pending the outcome of an inquiry, Walker resigned from the Army. Walker instantly became the martyr of the radical right because of his persecution by the Kennedy administration. It was later found that his right wing anti-communist teaching was encouraged by JCS Chairman General Lemnitzer.

In late October 1961, during an otherwise cordial luncheon at the White House for a group of publishers from Texas, the President, after a few casual remarks, opened the floor to questions. Ted Dealey,[vi] publisher of the Dallas Morning News and ardent supporter

---

[vi] His was the newspaper that, on the morning of the assassination, published the John Birch Society's full-page advertisement, "Welcome Mr. Kennedy to Dallas," criticizing the President. Dealey said that before agreeing to run the JBS ad, he had read it carefully and approved it because it accurately expressed the editorial opinion of the Dallas Morning News.

of the John Birch Society, seized the opportunity to read a prepared statement assailing the President saying,

> . . . we need a man on horseback to lead this nation and many people in Texas and the Southwest think that you are riding Carolyn's tricycle. The general opinion of the grass roots thinking in this country is that you and your administration are weak sisters . . . . We can annihilate Russia and should make that clear to the Soviet government . . . [48]

Clearly irritated, the President responded brusquely,

> Wars are easier to talk about than they are to fight. I have the responsibility for the lives of 180 million Americans, which you have not. I'm just as tough as you are, Mr. Dealey. I didn't get elected president by arriving at soft judgments.

As Dealey spewed his verbal tirade in Washington, the President's mind was undoubtedly elsewhere. Because, at that precise moment in Berlin, Soviet and American tanks were facing-off across the East German border at Checkpoint Charlie.

Operation Mongoose—1962

After the President's decision that troops were not going to Vietnam, Lansdale was re-assigned to something more in line with his expertise. Seven months after the Bay of Pigs disaster, the Kennedy administration, realizing that the Cuban problem was not going away, developed a new program to unseat Castro, code-named "Operation Mongoose." The plan consisted of a series of covert actions to destabilize Castro by subversion and sabotage and promote an internal uprising to help the Cubans overthrow Castro.

The plan consisted of five phases that were staged to foment internal revolt inside Cuba. These plans included economic warfare, psychological warfare, and sabotage activities, which would be followed by the injection of agents to organize an internal revolt. Lansdale added provisions to his plan that once a revolt had been instigated, it would be supported by direct military intervention by the United States.

Lansdale's program schedule was based on the revolt occurring during the first two weeks of October, followed by the establishment of a government "that the U.S. could live in peace with" during the last two weeks of October.

False Flags[vii]–Operation Northwoods–March 1962

> Although no one in Congress could have known it at the time, Lemnitzer and the Joint Chiefs had quietly slipped over the edge.[49]
>
> James Bamford, "Body of Secrets"

When President Eisenhower, his former commanding General, submitted his name as the next Chairman of the Joint Chiefs of Staff, Lyman Lemnitzer presented Congress with a lengthy curriculum vitae, emphasizing his expertise as a "consummate planner."[50] He took pride in his reputation as an outstanding strategist, which had been his forte over his entire military career. But, after only eight months as Chairman, he found himself under sharp criticism from the new Commander-in-Chief for the poor planning that produced the Bay of Pigs. From Lemnitzer's perspective, this critique would be especially galling because, while he planned the Allied invasions of North Africa and Sicily for Eisenhower, this new president, then a navy lieutenant, could not even manage to keep his tiny PT boat out of the way of a slower moving Japanese destroyer.

In the aftermath of the failed Cuban invasion, Kennedy issued new orders placing the JCS in charge of planning Cold War, i.e. covert, operations. The JCS Chairman evidently accepted the challenge with vigor, and focused his planning know-how to create a series of covert actions for use in the Cold War project that mattered to him most.

[vii] These are covert operations designed to deceive in such a way that the operations appear as though they are being carried out by other entities. The Nazis conducted one of the more notorious of these in 1939 when they set fire to the German Parliament building, known as the Reichstag, and blamed the communists. Hitler used the Reichstag Fire to demand that the government grant him emergency powers, with which he seized control of the country.

During the debate over sending combat troops to Vietnam, Kennedy asked the Chiefs why we should send American troops to fight communism ten thousand miles away, when we did not send them into Cuba, only ninety miles away.

The President asked how he could justify the proposed course of action in Vietnam while at the same time ignoring Cuba. General Lemnitzer hastened to add that the JCS feel even at this point we should go into Cuba.[51]

Lemnitzer's retort appears as a pointed answer expressing the bitterness that the military still felt because of the President's failure to use American military force during the Bay of Pigs. But it was more than that; it was a plain statement of fact. The Pentagon had become almost maniacal in their determination to excise the malignancy growing so close to the United States of America.

The General submitted his latest strategy for the liberation of Cuba to Robert McNamara for approval in March 1962. The plan, supported by all of the other Chiefs, consisted of a sequence of False-Flag operations, which they called "Operation Northwoods." These were intended to dovetail with Operation Mongoose, so that just when an internal Cuban revolt began, these operations would give the U.S. a pretext for an invasion.

Some of these plans included a significant amount of intricate military planning, Lemnitzer's specialty. The attacks he had planned included using friendly forces dressed as Cubans to attack the American military base at Guantanamo, or blowing up a U.S. ship in Cuban waters and blaming Cuba, or sinking a boatload of Cubans enroute to Florida. He also suggested developing a Communist Cuban terror campaign against American citizens in the Miami area, other Florida cities and Washington, coupled with the explosion of a few plastic bombs, followed by the arrest of Cuban agents carrying falsified documents indicating Cuban involvement.

But JFK was not about to approve a plan that included the wanton murder of ordinary citizens in order to provoke an attack on Cuba which the Soviets would likely counter with a strike at Berlin. Shortly after this plan was submitted, Kennedy decided to replace Lyman Lemnitzer as Chairman of the Joint Chiefs of Staff with Maxwell Taylor.

The Cuban Missile Crisis—October 1962

In April 1962, two and a half years after the two countries agreed to install them, U.S. Jupiter missiles finally became operational in Turkey. It is purported that, during a vacation in the Crimea that same month, Nikita Khrushchev gazed across the Black Sea towards Turkey and mulled over the possibility of sending Soviet missiles to Cuba in response to the American missiles now positioned along his border. When he returned to the Kremlin to discuss the proposal, he came up with two more reasons to go ahead with the plan. The first was that it could deter the U.S. attack on Cuba. An American invasion was expected in the fall, because Castro's agents were well aware of Operation Mongoose and Operation Northwoods. The second was to help close the weapons gap between the U.S.S.R. and the U.S. The Cubans estimated that in the event of an American attack, they could hold out for three to four days. It would take the Soviet Union longer than that to come to their assistance. The missiles would either deter the attack, or provide sufficient firepower until the Russians could respond. Advisors Andrei Gromoyko and Anastas Mikoyan warned Khrushchev that it was a "very dangerous step" that would cause a "political explosion" in the United States. Khrushchev proceeded, "over the concerns of the two of his advisors who knew American politics best,"[52] because he believed they could be installed before the Americans found out about them. Khrushchev planned to deliver a letter to JFK after the Congressional mid-term elections announcing the missile installation as a fait accompli.

All through the summer of 1962, the CIA reported that Soviet arms shipments to Cuba were increasing. The U.S. had noticed a significant surge in the number of Soviet ships off-loading cargo in Cuban ports. By late August, there were reports from senate committees of "rocket installations" in Cuba.

On Sunday, October 14, Major Richard S. Heyser flew the Air Force's first U-2 mission over the western section of Cuba and photographed areas where refugees reported that major construction was underway.

On previous flights by the CIA, Surface-to-Air Missile (SAM) sites had been detected, and the Soviets acknowledged that they were providing 'defensive' weapons to Cuba. A month earlier, the President formally warned the Russians that installation of 'offensive' weapons in Cuba would not be acceptable. The Soviet ambassador had provided assurances that the Soviet Union does not need to export their missiles to Cuba, since their rockets were so powerful, they can reach anywhere in the world. But it would soon be discovered that the Soviets were hiding behind semantics, because the photographs taken by Major Heyser showed Soviet Medium Range Missile sites under construction.

National Security Advisor Mac Bundy received the reconnaissance information at the White House late on Monday but waited until the next day to notify JFK. As soon as he was informed, the President assigned a special committee to work out the American response. This group was later dubbed the Executive Committee of the National Security Council, or ExComm, for short. The President decided that all members should maintain their schedules so that no one in the press would detect any unusual activity, to allow time to develop a strategy without tipping off the Russians. Rather than cancel at the last minute, JFK kept an appointment in Chicago for the same reason, although he came back a day early, claiming to have caught a cold.

One of the early pieces of advice that the President received was in the form of a memo from UN Ambassador Adlai Stevenson. In order to get the Soviets to remove their missiles, Stevenson advocated exchanging them for U.S. missiles in Turkey and Italy, and surrender of our military base in Guantanamo Bay. Kennedy rejected this, believing that their missiles could only be removed by military force. The discussions of the ExComm were mixed, some favored air strikes, others favored blockade. Air strikes could not guaranty getting all of the missiles, while a blockade would remove no missiles and allow construction to continue. Other advisors countered Stevenson:

> Dean Acheson came in our meeting and said that he felt that we should knock out the Soviet missiles in Cuba by air strike. Someone asked him, 'If we do, what do you think the

Soviet Union will do?' He said, 'I know the Soviet Union very well. I know what they are required to do in light of their history and their posture around the world. I think they will knock out our missiles in Turkey.' 'What do we do then?' he was asked. 'I believe under our NATO treaty, with which I was associated, we would be required to respond by knocking out a missile base in the Soviet Union,' Acheson went on. 'Then what do they do?' 'That is when we hope,' Acheson replied, 'that cooler heads will prevail, and they'll stop and talk.'[53]

On Thursday, Kennedy kept a previously scheduled appointment with Soviet Foreign Minister Andrei Gromoyko. During their meeting, the President, without revealing what he knew, asked the Foreign Minister some pointed questions about Soviet supply of offensive weapons to Cuba. Gromoyko gave his full assurances the "the Soviet Union would never become involved in such assistance." The President then reiterated his statement of September 13:

If at any time the Communist build-up in Cuba were to endanger or interfere with our security in any way, including our base at Guantanamo, our passage to the Panama Canal, our missile and space activities At Cape Canaveral, or the lives of American citizens in this country, or if Cuba should ever attempt to export its aggressive purposes by force or the threat of force against any nation in this hemisphere, or become an offensive military base of significant capacity for the Soviet Union, then this country will do whatever must be done to protect its own security and that of its allies.[54]

By Friday, the Joint Chiefs of Staff demanded immediate military action. They were anxious to strike at Cuba, especially LeMay who had been preparing for just such an opportunity for years. He felt there was no better time than the present. "We are prepared and 'the bear' is not."[55]

The Russian bear has always been eager to stick his paw in Latin American waters. Now we've got him in a trap, let's take his leg off right up to his testicles. On second thought, let's take off his testicles too! [56]

JFK believed that the Soviets might respond to a U.S. attack on Cuba by striking at Berlin. In ExComm meetings, the following exchange took place between the President and General LeMay:[57]

LeMay: Now as for the Berlin situation, I don't share your view that if we knock off Cuba, they're going to knock off Berlin. We've got the Berlin problem staring us in the face anyway. If we don't do anything to Cuba then they're going to push on Berlin, and push *real hard* because they've got us on the run. If we take military action against Cuba, then I think that the . . .

JFK: What do you think their reprisal would be?

LeMay: I don't think they're going to make any reprisal if we tell them that the Berlin situation is just like it's always been. If they make a move we're going to fight. Now I don't think this changes the Berlin situation at all, except that you've got to make one more statement on it.

So I see no other solution. This blockade and political action I see leading us to war. I don't see any other solution for it. It will lead right into war. This is almost as bad as the *appeasement at Munich.* [pause]

[Emphasis added]

Because if this [unclear] blockade comes along, their MiGs are going to fly. The IL-28s are going to fly against us. And we're going to gradually drift into a war under conditions that are at great disadvantage to us, with missiles staring us straight in the face, that can knock out our airfields in the southern portion [of the United States]. And if they use nuclear weapons, it's the population down there. We just drift into a war under conditions that we don't like. I just don't see any other solution except direct military action *right now.*

Comparing the proposed quarantine to the Appeasement at Munich was a clear attempt to goad the President by referring to his father's support of Chamberlin. After the meeting, JFK asked Kenny O'Donnell,

> Can you imagine LeMay saying a thing like that? These brass hats have one great advantage in their favor. If we listen to them, and do what they want us to do, none of us will be alive later to tell them that they were wrong. [58]

Over the weekend, the U.S. prepared to take its case to the Organization of American States (OAS) and the UN. It also mobilized troops and prepared for a blockade of Cuba. All of this activity drew the attention of the press corps. The President personally requested them to hold off with the story until he made a formal announcement. On Monday night, JFK made a televised address to the nation, announcing a 'quarantine' of Cuba and called on the Soviets to remove their missiles. At the same time, he raised the military defense position to DEFCON 3, just two levels below DEFCON 1; War.

The next day Khrushchev responded, rejecting the United States demand to remove the missiles, claiming the U.S. had no right to interfere in the relations between sovereign nations. Meanwhile, the OAS voted unanimously for a 'quarantine' of Cuba.

That quarantine became effective on Wednesday, October 24, and the military began to push the situation towards war. That same day, the military defense position was raised another level, to DEFCON 2, without presidential approval. These orders were issued by SAC Commander General Tommy Powers as an unencrypted transmission to make sure the Soviets got it. No one identified who ordered him to take this step, but Powers had to have had at least tacit permission from the JCS to do this.[59]

When the quarantine took effect, Admiral Anderson tried to fire warning shots across the bows of Soviet ships, and when McNamara stopped him Anderson argued that the navy does not need him to tell them how to do their job, because they've been running blockades since the days of "John Paul Jones.[60]" In early 2012, the John F. Kennedy Library released a tape recording of a conversation between Defense Secretary Robert McNamara and President Kennedy recorded just days before his trip to Dallas.

McNamara: I talked to [Admiral] Rickover in connection with this nuclear carrier and while we were discussing it, he said, 'You know that Anderson was absolutely insubordinate during the Cuban Crisis. He consciously acted contrary to the President's instructions. I just thought you'd be interested. Rickover told me ten days ago."

JFK: I wonder what he means . . .

McNamara: Well I didn't want to probe too much, I didn't want to have a discussion but, I just was—he was objecting, Rickover said enough to let me know that Anderson was objecting to the instructions that you and I were giving relating to the quarantine and the limiting of action in relation to stopping the Russian ships.

JFK: He wanted to sink a ship.

McNamara: He wanted to sink a ship. That's right.

As the crisis progressed, the Russians came to the realization that the U.S. Military was trying to provoke a nuclear war.[61] The following day SAC bombers flew past their fail-safe points. The story later spread that this is what caused Soviet ships to turnaround:

> SAC airborne alert bombers deliberately flew past their turnaround points towards soviet airspace. An unambiguous threat that Russian radar operators would have recognized and reported. The Bombers only turned around when the soviet vessels carrying missiles to Cuba stopped dead in the Atlantic.[62]

Although the bombers did fly past their hold points, the truth is that Khrushchev had already ordered Soviet vessels to turn around the day after Kennedy's address. Soviet ships were already sailing away from the quarantine line when this incident occurred.

Another provocative incident took place the next morning when a test missile was launched from Vandenberg Air Force Base at 4:00 AM in the general direction of the U.S.S.R., which they could have interpreted as a U.S. attack.[63] These incidents demonstrate the extent to which the American military was going to trigger a Soviet response.

Adlai Stevenson confronted Soviet Ambassador Zorin at the UN General Assembly as to whether or not the Soviet Union was installing missiles in Cuba. After Zorin refused to answer, saying the U.S. had no proof, Stevenson presented blowups of the detailed U-2 photographs.

Nikita Khrushchev sent a long passionate letter to the President on the morning of October 26, in which he offered to remove the missiles in exchange for an assurance that the U.S. would remove the quarantine and not invade Cuba. Similar terms had also been discussed through back channels between ABC correspondent John Scali and the Soviet Embassy's Aleksander Fomin. The ExComm was in the midst of preparing a response to this letter when a second letter was received from Khrushchev on Saturday, October 27. This second letter was more belligerent, and added a requirement that the U.S. missiles in Turkey must be removed as part of the settlement. Kennedy's advisors believed that hard-liners in the Kremlin had gotten to Khrushchev and may have possibly taken over, or that this was a ploy stalling for time to allow the technicians to finish work on the missile sites.

The legend later arose, referred to as the 'Trollope Ploy Myth,' that a decision was made to answer Khrushchev's first letter and ignore the second. In fact, the ExComm did draft and approve an official response to Khrushchev, accepting the terms of the previous letter, but after the meeting concluded, JFK asked certain members to stay, telling the others that the side meeting was to discuss an oral message to be delivered with the official letter, to amplify its contents. Those attending the smaller meeting with the President included Dean Rusk, Robert McNamara, Mac Bundy, George Ball, Roswell Gilpatric, Llewellyn Thompson, Ted Sorenson, and Robert Kennedy. RFK was instructed to tell Soviet Ambassador Dobrynin that while there could be no 'quid pro quo', the U.S. had already planned to remove these missiles, and that they would be removed in about six months, after things had cooled off. However, if the Soviets made this public, the President would deny it. In either event, the President had to have an answer within twenty-four hours, not as an ultimatum, but as a matter of necessity. The military was planning to begin air strikes on Monday. RFK met with the Soviet Ambassador, delivered the message, and according to Khrushchev's memoirs, Dobrynin reported that RFK also told him that:

> We're spending all day and night at the White House; I don't know how much longer we can hold out against our generals.[64]

Meanwhile an Air Force U-2 'strayed' over Siberia. Khrushchev complained to Kennedy "that an intruding American plane could be easily taken for a nuclear bomber which might push us to a fateful step."[65] Perhaps that was the military's intent. The President endeavored to do the opposite; prevent an unintended incident from starting general war. As the military prepared for invasion, a U-2 flight gathering the latest reconnaissance was shot down over Cuba, and the pilot, Major Rudolf Anderson, was killed. The ExComm debated: was this related to the hard-line response from the Kremlin? After consideration, Kennedy concluded that this was an isolated incident; that Khrushchev did not intend to start a war, he, therefore, cancelled the counterstrike. The Pentagon was preparing that retaliatory strike when orders came from the White House to cancel it. The Pentagon was stunned:

> LeMay was admonished not to launch the aircraft until he received direct orders from the President. Angered, LeMay hung up. "He chickened out again. How in the hell do you get men to risk their lives when the SAMs are not

attacked?" When an aid said he would wait at the phone for the President's order, LeMay disgustedly said, "It will never come!"[66]

On October 28, the United States advised its NATO allies that a military attack on Cuba was imminent. The CIA learned that in the past twenty-four hours, all twenty-four medium range missile sites in Cuba had been made operational. However, no nuclear bunkers appeared to be in operation. The CIA concluded that the missiles were not armed.

Early that morning U.S. radar picked up an apparent missile launch from Cuba with a Tampa trajectory, which was discovered, only after the projected impact did not happen, to be a computer test tape.[67]

Less than twelve hours after RFK's meeting with Dobrynin, a Radio Moscow broadcast announced that the Soviets will remove the missiles in return for a pledge from the U.S. never to invade Cuba. The immediate crisis had passed.

The Military were livid. When JFK thanked the JCS for their help in winning, LeMay exploded, "Won hell! This is the worst defeat in our history! We should knock 'em off tomorrow!" Admiral Anderson told the President "We've been had!"[68] and LeMay chewed Kennedy out.[69] JFK came to the conclusion that "the military are mad, they wanted to do this."[70]

Even after the Russian announcement, the JCS, led by LeMay, sent the President a letter recommending execution of the planned air strikes followed by invasion unless there was "direct irrefutable evidence" of immediate Soviet action to remove the missile sites. The Chiefs also insisted that the US invade unless the Soviets remove the IL-28 bombers. This issue extended final negotiations by almost a month, until Khrushchev finally agreed to remove the planes. At a press conference on November 20, 1962, JFK announced that the Soviets had agreed to remove their IL-28 bombers from Cuba and therefore, the US will end the quarantine. He confirmed this in a formal letter to Khrushchev, which he signed the next day, officially ending the Cuban Missile Crisis.

After the collapse of the Soviet Union, a series of five conferences was held amongst surviving members of the ExComm, the former Soviet Union, and Cuba, to discuss and reconstruct the events surrounding the Cuban Missile Crisis of 1962. These conferences were particularly elucidating because all sides could openly discuss the decisions that were made during the crisis and learn facts which they could not have known at the time, directly from the principals. All participants came to the realization that all three sides had acted based on a significant amount of incorrect information and erroneous assumptions that led to serious misjudgments. The incident will be studied by historians for years to come.

The American University—June 1963

The 49th graduating class of the American University has the singular distinction of having been the audience for the most significant speech delivered by John F. Kennedy during his tenure as president. In the aftermath of the Cuban Missile Crisis, JFK believed that there was an opportunity to improve relations with the Soviet Union as both sides realized how close they had come to the abyss. He wanted to use this speech to extend an olive branch to Khrushchev to prepare the way for negotiating a nuclear test ban treaty. The speech itself was kept confidential and only Bundy, Sorenson and a few of the President's closest advisers knew about it as it developed that spring. It was kept so secret that it was not given to the State Department or the Pentagon for review until two days prior to the June 10 commencement ceremony. In examining the contents of this speech, we find little with which the Pentagon would not have taken issue.

After a few introductory remarks, the President introduces 'peace' as the subject of his talk, and begins with the rhetorical question:

> What kind of peace do I mean and what kind of a peace do we seek? Not a *Pax Americana* enforced on the world by American weapons of war. Not the peace of the grave or the security of the slave. I am talking about genuine peace, the kind of peace that makes life on earth worth living, and the kind that enables men and nations to grow, and to hope, and build a better life for their children—not merely peace for Americans but peace for all men and women, not merely peace in our time, but peace in all time.

His listeners may not have recognized the phrasing, but these opening lines were a direct rebuttal of LeMay's oft-stated position. In his military lectures LeMay frequently compared America's military power to what was once Rome's *Pax Romana,* and later England's *Pax Britannica,* and now SAC had become what he initially labeled *Pax Atomica,* but in recent addresses, had actually begun referring to as *Pax Americana.*[71] And the last part of this opening is an amalgam of Neville Chamberlin's pronouncement after the Munich agreement, along with phrasing used by Woodrow Wilson. Any allusion by JFK to Chamberlin likely invoked unpleasant reminders of his father's support of appeasement.

Then, after encouraging the leaders of the Soviet Union to adopt a more enlightened attitude towards peace, he asks Americans to

> . . . reexamine our attitude towards the Soviet Union. It is discouraging to think that their leaders may actually believe what their propagandists write. It is discouraging to read a recent, authoritative Soviet text on military strategy and find, on page after page, wholly baseless and incredible claims, such as the allegation that American imperialist circles are preparing to unleash different types of war, that there is a very real threat of a preventive war being unleashed by American imperialists against the Soviet Union, and that the political aims—and I quote—"of the American imperialists are to enslave economically and politically the European and other capitalist countries and to achieve world domination by means of aggressive war."

Considering the Net Evaluation Subcommittee's report and the SIOP-62 briefing, JFK knew full well that those Soviet textbooks were precisely correct; the American military had been planning a pre-emptive strike for years. But his successful conclusion of the Cuban missile crisis had convinced Kennedy that he now had full control of the military. In a televised interview with CBS news in mid-December 1962, he was asked:

> Mr. President, your predecessor, President Eisenhower, in his farewell message to the people just before he left office, warned of the dangers of a possible military-industrial complex that might threaten the very nature of democracy. Have you felt this threat at all while you are [sic] in office?

To which the President replied:

> Well, it seems to me that there was probably more of that
> feeling *perhaps some months ago than I would say today.*[72]
> [Emphasis added]

And by refuting the things which the Soviet Premier and the American president both know the Pentagon had been planning, Kennedy was signaling to Khrushchev that he now had reined-in the military, has put a stop to the pre-emptive strike plan and is proceeding with his own agenda.

Also notable throughout the speech, in direct contrast to the customary American demonization of the Soviet Union, the President instead emphasized our common ground, encouraging his audience to change their perception of the Soviets and to see them as fellow human beings. He acknowledged the millions of deaths and the wreckage of their country as a result of the Second World War, putting their losses into perspective with what it would have meant to the United States; a "loss equivalent to the devastation of this country east of Chicago." And contrary to the "CONTAINMENT" and "ROLL-BACK" policies of the preceding two administrations, he urges that we instead learn to live with the communists.

> So let us not be blind to our differences, but let us also
> direct attention to our common interests and the means by
> which those differences can be resolved. And if we cannot
> end now our differences, at least we can help make the
> world safe for diversity. For in the final analysis, our most
> basic common link is that we all inhabit this small planet.
> We all breathe the same air. We all cherish our children's
> futures. And we are all mortal.

But to the military in general, and to LeMay in particular, the most egregious part of the speech would have been what followed. The President announced that he was proceeding with his oft-stated objective of negotiating a comprehensive Test Ban Treaty with the Soviet Union. This would be the first stage in achieving the ultimate goal of "general and complete disarmament." Furthermore, he pronounced that the United States would unilaterally cease the testing of nuclear weapons in the atmosphere "so long as other states do not do so."

It is small wonder why the speech was not shown to the Pentagon until only days before. The military believed that they had struggled mightily since the end of the war to achieve the definitive military advantage that the U.S. held over the communists. And now, without consulting the organization whose duty it was to defend the country, and who built a vast nuclear arsenal to do it, he was going to squander that advantage. The military believed that this was too big of a decision for him to make on his own.

Finally, in closing, Kennedy reiterates the message that the pre-emptive strike plans were finished:

> The United States, as the world knows, will never start a war. We do not want a war . . . . Confident and unafraid, we labor on—not toward a strategy of annihilation but toward a strategy of peace.

It was, therefore, extremely plausible for Knebel to base his plot for *Seven Days in May* around the signing of a Test Ban Treaty with the Soviet Union. In his novel, it was this treaty that lead his fictional General Scott to plan the overthrow of his imaginary President Lyman. The real-life military was dead-set against a Test Ban Treaty because they believed the Russians would cheat, and after we had stopped our program, would secretly continue theirs and test new weapons surreptitiously. When asked how they could possibly cheat, since atmospheric nuclear tests were easily detected, LeMay exclaimed, "They'll test behind the moon!"

Making the argument for both sides, Khrushchev called the American University speech the best ever made by an American president, and allowed its uncensored re-broadcast over Radio Moscow. During that summer, negotiations proceeded and an agreement on a limited test ban treaty was reached with the Soviet Union. It was signed in Moscow in August and ratified by the U.S. Senate in September 1963, over the barely muted complaints of the Joint Chiefs of Staff.

Withdrawal from Vietnam—October 1963

After the 'Thanksgiving Day Massacre,' Kennedy asked his remaining advisors who would be personally responsible for Vietnam. McNamara answered that himself and "L" (Lemnitzer) would take charge of the war.

McNamara paid close attention, holding monthly SECDEF (Secretary of Defense) conferences with military leaders sometimes in Honolulu and other times in Siagon. But something strange began to take place. The military estimates received by McNamara and the President were falsified. The enemy strength was grossly underestimated, and the South Vietnamese army's successes were grossly overstated. The picture painted for McNamara at each of these conferences throughout 1962 and 1963 was that the war was being won. However, the truth was that the Viet Cong were making great strides and the people were turning against the government. The South Vietnamese army actually avoided contact with the communists and would call in air strikes instead, because Diem would punish his generals if they suffered any casualties. Consequently, the advisors that Kennedy sent were taking on ever increasing combat roles. In addition, many of the supposed Viet Cong casualties were actually innocent civilians killed by American bombing. The reason for the false stories was because if the President knew what the situation really was, he would likely withdraw the advisors because they were not helping.

But something else unusual was taking place at the same time. After LBJ had shown support for Burke's recommendation for sending troops to Laos, through his military aide, Colonel Howard Burris, Vice President Johnson was receiving accurate reports throughout 1962 and 1963. Only he was hearing the truth.

But by March 1963, the President had apparently figured out the deception and decided to use it to his advantage. If the war was going as well as the military was reporting, then we could turn it over to the South Vietnamese army and the U.S. could withdraw American advisors, since they had apparently done their job. That is where the discussion of the withdrawal of 1,000 advisors initiated. McNamara told the military to start planning for full withdraw in three years. The units we sent home would be replaced with South Vietnamese army units trained by U.S. advisors. In October 1963, the White House announced that 1,000 advisors could be withdrawn from Vietnam. Kenny O'Donnell recalled that after Senator Mike Mansfield visited Vietnam and criticized the President about his involvement there that

> Later the President asked me to invite Mike Mansfield into his office for a private talk on the problem. I sat in for part of the discussion. The President told Mansfield that he had been having second thoughts about Mansfield's argument and that he now agreed with the Senator's thinking on the need for a complete military withdrawal from Vietnam. "But I can't do it until 1965—after I'm reelected," Kennedy told Mansfield. President Kennedy explained, and Mansfield agreed with him, that if he announced a withdrawal of American military personnel before the 1964 election, there would be a wild conservative outcry against returning him to the Presidency for a second term.[73]

O'Donnell said that Kennedy reiterated this to him later

> After Mike Mansfield left the office, the President said to me, "In 1965, I'll become one of the most unpopular Presidents in history. I'll be dammed everywhere as a Communist appeaser. But I don't care. If I tried to pull out completely now from Vietnam we would have another Joe McCarthy scare on our hands, but I can do it after I'm reelected. So we had better make damn sure I *am* reelected.[74]

At the same time, Diem was becoming even more repressive which was worsening the war effort and making Kennedy's withdrawal plan more difficult. Buddhist discontent with Diem's pro-Catholic discrimination erupted in 1963 following the banning of the Buddhist flag and shootings at the Hue Vesak temple. This resulted in a series of mass demonstrations during what became known as the 'Buddhist Crisis' in which monks were setting themselves on fire in protest of the government's policies. With Diem unwilling to bend, his brother Nhu orchestrated the Xa Loi Pagoda raids, which killed protestors by the hundreds. As a result, America's relationship with Diem broke down and eventually the U.S. encouraged a military coup in which Diem was killed.

The whole time Johnson was kept up to date with the actual situation, and rather than withdrawal, he and the military wanted to commit combat troops. The President was the only one standing in their way. On November 21, the same day that President Kennedy left Washington on his way to Texas, his National Security Advisor, Mac Bundy, left the latest Vietnam conference in Honolulu and rushed back to the White House to prepare a draft of NSAM 273. The subject of this new directive was American policy in Vietnam. The draft paragraph number 2 rephrases the withdraw of American troops from Vietnam, announced in a White house statement on October 2, as an 'objective,' and the remainder of the document is exactly opposite to JFK's previous directions and stated policy regarding South Vietnam. Why would Bundy hurry back to Washington to draft instructions that JFK would be unlikely to approve? As this was the day before the assassination, it begs the question; did "the President" in this NSAM refer to the 35th or the 36th? Taken literally, the first sentence of paragraph number 4 is exceptionally bizarre:

> It is of the highest importance that the United States Government avoid either the appearance or the reality of public recrimination from one part of it against another, and the President expects that all senior officers of the Government will take energetic steps to insure that they and their subordinates go out of their way to maintain and to defend the unity of the United States Government both here and in the field.

Why would a President of the United States suddenly find it necessary to instruct senior officers and subordinates to go out of their way to maintain and to defend the unity of the United States Government against public recrimination? Were these instructions prepared in case something went wrong in Dallas the next day? Note that in the version of this document signed by Johnson the day after Kennedy's funeral, this paragraph had drastically changed. The unity of the United States government was no longer in question, and there was a complete turn-around in the U.S. Government's policy regarding Vietnam.

> The President expects that all senior officers of the Government will move energetically to ensure the full unity of support for established U.S. policy in South Vietnam. Both in Washington and in the field, it is essential that the Government be unified. It is of particular importance that express or implied criticism of officers of other branches be scrupulously avoided in all contacts with the Vietnamese Government and with the press. More specifically, the President approves the following lines of action developed in the discussions of the Honolulu meeting of November 20. The offices of the Government to which central responsibility is assigned are indicated in each case.

Closing Argument

———————•———————

Out of all of the events that occurred during the Kennedy administration, which of them would have incited the military to murder the President?

There are a number of possibilities, and an answer is not immediately obvious. The Chiefs questioned his mettle after he refused to send in American forces at the Bay of Pigs, and even pondered his removal then, and that was only three months after he took office. They were angry at his refusal to follow their recommendation to send American troops into Laos, where he instead accepted a coalition government with the communists. They were disturbed at what they viewed as his 'weak' performance in Vienna followed by his indecisiveness during the Berlin crisis, and his unwillingness to confront Khrushchev over construction of the Berlin Wall. There are indications that they may have even considered demolishing the wall on their own. Then, in the face of blatant 'communist aggression' in Vietnam, he repeatedly refused to send U.S. combat troops. And to make matters worse, he was maneuvering to withdraw the American military advisors. When the clandestine installation of Soviet missiles in Cuba was discovered, he refused the Joint Chiefs' strident demands for an invasion. And less than a year later, he pushed through a Test Ban Treaty, which required us to trust the very same country that had just attempted to sneak their missiles into Cuba. In summary, the United States Military had reached the conclusion that this president was never going to stand up to communism, and to the Soviet Union in particular, a nation that they were absolutely certain would leap at the first opportunity to wipe us off the face of the earth. In short, from the Military's point of view, President Kennedy was a coward.

Recent thought, initiated largely by John Newman's excellent work, *JFK and Vietnam*, is that Kennedy's planned withdrawal from

Vietnam is what precipitated his murder. And Newman presents a strong argument, because American action in that country certainly did a dramatic about-face after his death. And just three weeks prior to the President's assassination, South Vietnam's own President Diem and his brother died in a bloody coup carried out by their military. Many believe that the assassination of both leaders were part of military coups in each country, removing obstacles at either end so that the war in Vietnam could proceed in earnest.

Kennedy's Vietnam policy was a significant factor in the Military's desire to eliminate the President, but it was not their only reason. In the numerous crises during his administration after the Bay of Pigs, Kennedy sought to circumvent, bypass or otherwise marginalize the advice of the military. The Chiefs complained about JFK's tendency to appoint a Task Force or a committee to address issues involving the use of force rather than accept their advice without question. He had relegated them to an advisory role, whereas, in every other administration since World War II, they had a more direct decision-making position. JFK stopped General Clay's actions in Berlin, and he had failed to take the military action they had prescribed in Laos, Vietnam, and Cuba.

While it was all of the President's policies in general, the Prosecution submits that it was one of his actions, in particular, that pushed them over the edge. It was the straw that broke the camel's back. Yet, this is the one episode that is generally overlooked in this regard, because it is widely considered, even by some of his critics, to be his finest hour; the Cuban Missile Crisis. You ladies and gentlemen of the jury may well ask, *'why would that be the one? He convinced Khrushchev to remove the missiles settling the crisis, and at the same time averted nuclear war. Why would this one be the reason?'*

The answer is that, considering all of the other cases, we see that, in each of them, the United States was in the position of helping some other nation defend itself against one communist threat or another; including assisting Cuban exiles against Castro. However, in none of them was the U.S. in any immediate danger. But when our sworn enemy installed their ballistic missiles in Cuba, they were directly threatening the American Homeland. In the last years of the Eisenhower administration, the *Gaither Report* warned that the most critical danger to the United States would be if the Soviet Union was ever able to launch a surprise attack against SAC facilities in the U.S. The missiles in Cuba gave the Soviet Union precisely that capability. And a threat to SAC was a threat to its former Commander, the Defendant, Curtis E. LeMay. In one move, the U.S.S.R. had turned the tables on the U.S., so that all of the years of preparation, and all of those strategic advantages vanished. Yet, in the face of such a provocative threat, this President refused to order what they considered the appropriate military action.

But, there is a particular reason why the missile crisis is not immediately recognized as the genesis of the murder plot. That is because for a long time certain critical facts were withheld from the public. The third conference to study the Cuban Missile Crisis, held in Moscow in 1989, revealed a new and crucial detail. Participating in the conference was Anatoly Dobrynin, the former Soviet Ambassador with whom Robert Kennedy had met and to whom he delivered the President's letter, with his accompanying verbal message on October 27. Dobrynin's revelation at the Moscow conference was that, unbeknownst to any members of the ExComm, Bobby Kennedy met with him at the Soviet embassy in Washington late the previous night, Friday October 26. This occurred at the height of the crisis, after Khrushchev's first letter, but before his second. At this earlier meeting, when Dobrynin argued to Robert that the Soviet action in Cuba was no different from the U.S. Deployment of Jupiter Missiles in Turkey, RFK responded that the United States may be willing to remove the Turkish missiles as part of the deal. The Attorney General went out of the room to call his brother for confirmation, and returned shortly thereafter to verify that the President was ready to consider including the Turkish missiles in the deal.[75] Some now believe that this prior meeting between Dobrynin and RFK is the reason that the missile trade was incorporated in Khrushchev's second letter, and not that Khrushchev had been overridden by Soviet hard-liners, as many in the administration believed at the time. Also attending the conference was Ted Sorenson, who, in response to Dobrynin's new information, conceded that in his editing of

Robert Kennedy's notes for the posthumous publication of the book, *Thirteen Days*, he had changed the section about the Jupiter Missiles. Sorenson had deliberately obscured the fact that the removal of the Jupiter missiles in Turkey was very much part of the deal. But, in 1962, that detail had to be kept secret, as Dobrynin had then reported to Khrushchev:

> . . . the President can't say anything public in this regard about Turkey . . . his [Robert Kennedy's] comments about Turkey are extremely confidential; besides him and his brother, only 2-3 people know about it in Washington.[76]

Immediately afterward, rumors were rife in Washington that Kennedy had cut a secret deal with Khrushchev. When JFK called Eisenhower afterward to explain the settlement, the former president was astonished that the Russians would make what he considered such "an extremely conciliatory gesture." Based on the General's personal experience, it was highly out of character for the Russians to agree to remove their missiles without something more tangible in return. At the same time, Turkey was pressing the administration for confirmation that their missiles were not part of the settlement. And at the Pentagon, Robert McNamara told the JCS, somewhat disingenuously:

> . . . there was no Cuba-Turkey missile deal *at present*. [Emphasis added]

The growing rumors quickly pointed to one of the President's former political rivals when an article presenting the first account of the crisis appeared in the December issue of *The Saturday Evening Post*. Its author directly accused Adlai Stevenson of openly suggesting a missile trade, but reported that the President rejected it, which he did, at first. The article was written by Charlie Bartlett, who was known to be a personal friend of JFK, so many believed it was based on the President's direct input. It was not. It most likely came from the memo Stevenson sent to the President at the outset of the crisis. And although the White House reviewed the article before its publication, they did not add or detract. However, indicating his awareness that the missile trade would be viewed as appeasement, the President instructed Arthur Schlesinger to warn Stevenson that an article accusing him of "advocating a Caribbean Munich" was coming.[77]

And almost a year later, Kennedy's presumptive opponent in the 1964 presidential election, Arizona Senator Barry Goldwater, continued to raise the issue, alleging that there was more to the deal than had been made public, as exemplified in the following question to JFK during a presidential news conference in September 1963:

> Mr. President, in a Chicago speech last night [9/11/63], Senator Goldwater said *there are not ten men in America who know the full truth about Cuba*, all the facts of the test ban treaty *or the commitments made on behalf of this Nation with governments dedicated to our destruction.* He seems to be hinting that *you made secret agreements* both *in the Cuban settlement last fall,* and to obtain the test ban treaty.[78] [Emphasis added]

The President deftly confined his response to the test ban treaty aspect of the question, and sidestepped the implication regarding the Cuban settlement altogether.

So why, in the end, did JFK make the deal with our Jupiter missiles in Turkey? Bobby's exchange with Dobrynin was not the first time it came up. In the tape recordings of the ExComm meetings, as the crisis intensified, the President can be heard mulling over the various aspects of a potential missile exchange. The first conference to study the Cuban Missile Crisis revealed that if Khrushchev had not agreed to the offer he presented through his brother to Dobrynin, the President was prepared to have General Secretary U Thant propose the missile trade at the UN. Why? *Was* he a coward?

The answer depends entirely on what is meant by the question. If the question refers to physical courage, the answer is most definitely not. John Kennedy certainly did not fear for his personal safety. During the war, he had used his father's influence to get into the Navy, when he could have easily stayed home. The commendation accompanying his Navy medal cited his courage and leadership in saving his crew after his PT boat was rammed by the Japanese. Because of the back injuries received during this event, he later faced life-threatening surgery attempting to repair it. And, as has been well documented, because of other health issues, his longevity had been a question. Bobby famously joked about the risk a mosquito took by biting Jack. Kennedy himself had become fatalistic about death, even the possibility of assassination. Just before they left their hotel room in Fort Worth prior to departing for Dallas, he told his wife, "Jackie, if somebody wants to shoot me from a window with a rifle, nobody can stop it, so why worry about it?"

And if the question refers to a willingness to struggle against powerful opponents, where the stakes are high and the outcome uncertain, the answer is also no. This was evident when President battled several major steel companies in April 1962. Kennedy had persuaded the steelworkers union to accept wage limits in their contract to avoid an inflationary cycle. No sooner was the last labor contract signed, than several steel companies simultaneously announced a significant price increase. These companies had, in effect, used him to do their bidding with the unions in order to grab a large profit increase for themselves. The President risked the prestige of the office, and possibly his own re-election, to take on those companies, and fought until the price increase was rescinded.

However, for the best answer, the President should be measured by his own yardstick. Years before, JFK won a Pulitzer Prize for a book whose central topic focused on exactly what personal courage entailed. Written during his convalescence from his back surgery in 1954, *Profiles in Courage* tells the stories of eight U.S. Senators who embodied John Kennedy's definition of courage.[79] The common thread in each of the accounts is that each of these men had the moral courage to stand up for their principles, not just to their adversaries but, more significantly, to their associates and constituents. In many situations in life, it is frequently much easier for us as individuals to go along with the majority than it is to take an unpopular stand, but these men did, courageously facing the consequences. This is what JFK believed courage to be.

In the retrospective examination of the events of his administration, we see that JFK stood up to his contemporaries, by consistently resisting their repeated efforts to push the United States into war. These efforts came sometimes from his own advisors, but always from the military. In Laos, Cuba, Berlin, Vietnam, Cuba again, and Vietnam again, the Pentagon's solution to each situation was combat, yet it was always his last. This was the source of the conflict between the military and the President. As Arthur Schlesinger reported, "We [the Kennedy Administration] were at war with the national security people." So, once again the answer is no, JFK was not a coward.

Yet, as the President followed his principles, the Pentagon followed their own. However, in the nuclear age, in addition to the time-honored traditions of military valor, their definition of courage had evolved to include the most macabre requirement ever encountered in all of human experience. A modern president now had to be willing to push *THE* button in ordering an attack on the enemy's forces, knowing that in so doing, hundreds of millions of human beings would be exterminated. A horror to which the military had become completely immune. And, contrary to the cold-warrior rhetoric of his inaugural address, what the Pentagon found to be his reluctance to confront the communist threat convinced them that when the time came, the President would not have the courage to order a nuclear attack, even when it was absolutely necessary. Conversely, the two years of dealing with this cadre of military men and their plans, particularly their premeditated all-out tactical strike, convinced the President that when the time came, he would be the only person with the courage to stop a nuclear attack, *unless* it was absolutely necessary. He had to be the last resort. So, it is, finally, in this regard that, in living by his own standards, he failed to live up to theirs.

Moreover, where the military believed that any decision on the nuclear option was best delegated to professional soldiers, as Eisenhower had done, Kennedy had the temerity to believe that that decision was exclusively within the purview of the Commander-in-Chief. The Supreme Court concurred with JFK, as he pointed out in remarks at a political dinner in Camden, New Jersey in June 1960:

> In foreign affairs, said the Supreme Court, "The president alone has the power to speak or listen as the representative of the nation. The president alone."

> . . . He cannot share this power, he cannot delegate it, he cannot adjourn. He alone is the Chief of State, not the National Security Council, Vice President and all . . . . *He alone must decide what areas we defend—not the Congress, or the military, or the CIA,* and certainly not some beleaguered generalissimo on an island. [Emphasis added]

A famously voracious reader, the President in early 1962 consumed Barbara Tuchman's new book, *The Guns of August,* and it had a substantive effect on his thinking. Ms. Tuchman's work enumerated the many misjudgments and miscalculations made by early 20th century European leaders, which ultimately led to the First World War, and as she reveals, "wiped out an entire generation." The particularly tragic lesson she illuminates is that it was all a colossal waste that could have been avoided. So, forty-seven years later, with his sober responsibility as President of the United States, JFK was determined not to commit, or allow subordinates to commit, similar errors that could result in the Final World War, wiping out *all* generations. The President was determined to make decisions that controlled events, rather than allow events to control his decisions. And, while he was concerned about the Soviet response to our actions, he was equally concerned that his own military would overreact to the slightest Soviet movement.

So, in late October 1962, as American Armed Forces massed for an invasion of Cuba, JFK came face-to-face with what Mac Bundy termed the "moment of thermonuclear truth." The President needed to be absolutely certain that, before he started down a road which could later require him to issue that ultimate attack order, it had to be because our continued existence on this planet was threatened. And a dozen or so missiles in Turkey, which our own government knew to be complete junk, and which he already considered cancelling, did not pass muster. Eisenhower himself recognized that they were worthless when he planned to put them there in response to Sputnik. They were deployed for psychological effect only. Not vital to our tactical or our strategic arsenal, these missiles were outdated when the decision was made to send them, and by the time they were actually operational, they had been rendered obsolete by their Polaris submarine-launched replacements. They were scarecrows; they meant nothing to us. The Jupiters were expendable.

But, of course, the Russians would not know that, and to the military's way of thinking, having the them believe otherwise and agreeing to take them out under these circumstances was tantamount to surrender. In their opinion, JFK chose to appease the enemy, rather than to follow the advice of his own military. In the process, they believed he had also betrayed a NATO ally, and let the Soviets think we had acquiesced. Plus, JFK's non-invasion pledge effectively guaranteed that the U.S. would be assuring the preservation of a permanent communist foothold in the Western Hemisphere. This was the worst possible outcome, as LeMay, summarizing the military view, grumbled:

> I knew that yellow banty-legged bastard would fuck up the works! [80]

But this time around, it was far more serious than another denial of one more of the Joint Chief's never-ending demands for military action. There was fury within the military leadership in the aftermath of the missile crisis. In their minds, this time Kennedy's actions were criminal. In taking the oath of office, JFK had sworn to preserve, protect, and defend the Constitution of the United States. They believed he had broken that oath, by committing the one and only crime identified in that Constitution: Treason. Article III, Section 3, paragraph 1 defines it:

> Treason against the United States shall consist only in levying
> War against them, or in *adhering to their Enemies*, giving

them Aid and Comfort. No Person shall be convicted of
Treason unless on the Testimony of two Witnesses to the same
overt Act, or on Confession in open Court. [Emphasis added]

And even though the President managed to keep the missile trade
concealed from the public, he could not secrete it from the military,
who had their own like-minded witnesses. In 1963, the Supreme
Allied Commander of NATO was none other than former JCS
Chairman General Lyman Louis Lemnitzer, who Kennedy replaced
with Max Taylor just two weeks before the discovery of the missile
sites in Cuba. In his new Command, Lemnitzer would know how
deeply Turkey "resented their interests being traded-off to appease
an enemy", particularly without prior consultation. The Turks found
it "inexcusable to equate their role as a NATO partner with what they
saw as Cuba's 'stooge status' with the U.S.S.R."[81] So, when the Jupiter
missiles were actually dismantled, crated, and shipped back the
following April, Lemnitzer had to know that their removal was part
of the Cuban deal from the previous October. The Turks undoubtedly
voiced their displeasure, and he certainly would have communicated
this information back to the Pentagon.

There is a related common-law legal concept known as *misprision of
treason*, which stipulates that anyone who knows treason has been,
or is about to be committed, is duty-bound to do something about it.
In this case, according to Article II, Section 4 of the Constitution, the
"removal from office on impeachment for, and conviction of treason,
bribery, or other high crimes and misdemeanors" should have been
their remedy. However, impeachment in this case was not going to
be a viable option, because his purported treasonous act had been
deliberately concealed from the public, who was elated at the peaceful
outcome of the crisis. There would have been precisely zero public
support for his impeachment. Because they know impeachment is not
possible, and at the same time believing themselves duty-bound to
do something, they appoint themselves as judge and jury, and render
their verdict: guilty. The sentence: death.

But, unlike the French military's attempt to assassinate Charles
DeGaulle in August 1962, in which the assailants drove up close and

fired into his car, this would be a much more intricate plan, and one that would not be directly attributable to them. It is cruel irony that the President's assassination was planned by the military, because in so doing they were complying with his order of NSAM 55, directing the JCS to develop all future covert operations. This plan took some time to put into place. And who better to develop the details of an ultra-secret operation like this than the supreme planner himself, Lyman Lewis Lemnitzer. Credit for carrying out the intricate scheme is attributed to Special Operations expert General Edward Lansdale. He was certainly the right person, in the right position to do so:

> Lansdale, then an Air Force general working in the office of Special Operations for the Secretary of Defense, had a long history of experience in covert operations . . . he had powerful allies in the CIA, and his professional patron was the agency's Director, Allen Dulles. Lansdale even owed his promotion to Brigadier General to Dulles, who had intervened with Air Force Chief of Staff Curtis LeMay to bring it about.[82]

Lansdale is said to have used personnel from Mongoose, combined with other CIA assets, and turned the anti-Castro operation against the President. Lansdale resigned from the Air Force on November 1, 1963, which was, not coincidently, the day before the coup against his good friend Diem in Vietnam, and only three weeks before Kennedy's trip to Dallas. A telling photograph taken just after the assassination shows three alleged 'tramps'[83] in sheriffs' custody, walking East in single file past the Texas School Book Depository. These men had been arrested minutes after the shooting, when they were found in a boxcar in the rail yard behind the picket fence in Dealey Plaza. The picture also happens to capture the back of a well-dressed man walking in the opposite direction.[84] Several of the people who knew him best have identified that man as Ed Lansdale.[85]

As has been widely noted, shortly after the assassination, an unusually high number of the people connected to this case were themselves murdered, committed suicide, or otherwise died suddenly. Although a few of these cases do not raise suspicions, others definitely do. One of the latter is Guy Banister; the former FBI agent turned private investigator out of whose office Oswald promoted the *Fair Play for Cuba Committee*. Banister died under unusual circumstances in early June 1964, a little more than six months after the President's murder. What makes his case suspect is that he told an associate a few days before his death that, "If I'm dead in a week, no matter what the circumstances look like, it won't be from natural causes." A witness said he was shot through a window. The official version was that he died of a heart attack, alone.[86] Shortly after Banister's death, all of his files inexplicably disappeared from his office. However, New Orleans District Attorney Jim Garrison was able to retrieve a few of the items that remained, including the "Hands Off Cuba" pamphlets that Oswald was handing out when he was arrested in New Orleans, plus the index cards to Banister's missing files. Among the titles of those files were these:

-   American Central Intelligence Agency
-   Civil Rights Program of J.F.K.
-   Dismantling of Ballistic Missile System
-   *Missile Bases Dismantled—Turkey and Italy* [87] [Emphasis added]

These would be peculiar topics to keep files on if he were in fact just an ordinary private investigator. However, they take on a much more sinister implication knowing they belonged to a man closely associated with the intelligence agent later framed as the President's assassin.

There are myriad alternate theories as to why JFK was killed. These generally can be categorized by financial and/or personal gain as their motive, but each seems to benefit only a limited group of people, or in some cases, just certain individuals. Examples of the major ones include:

-   The profit to be made from a war in Vietnam; or
-   Defense appropriations such as for the TFX fighter jet; or
-   The revenue loss from Kennedy's plans to reduce the oil depletion allowance; or

- His alleged plan to change the Federal Reserve Bank system; or
- The money the mafia was losing at home because of RFK's persecution, and in Cuba because of Castro; or even
- LBJ's own presidential ambitions, compounded by his pressing need to avoid looming criminal prosecution

There is a principle known as *Occam's Razor* which is usefully applied when judging competing hypotheses that attempt to explain some data or event. The principle predicts that the correct hypothesis is the one that makes the fewest assumptions. In other words, the theory that is the truth is almost always the one that is the least complicated. In that regard, the explanations postulated above should be dismissed, because they are all too convoluted or their benefits too limited in scope to inspire others to take the risk inherent with becoming a participant in this conspiracy. If discovered, anyone involved in a plot like this would face execution, or long prison terms at least. We all remember that John Wilkes Booth shot Abraham Lincoln, but little mention is made about the four of his co-conspirators who were hanged shortly thereafter. Quite a number of people were involved in the 35th President's murder and its cover-up, yet none of the reasons listed above appears to be worth the personal danger that one would have to accept to carry it out, as well as to maintain secrecy forever. How many people would be willing to risk their lives to preserve the oil depletion allowance? Would the Pentagon decide to murder a president for money?

But, consider your own reaction at the mention of the name Benedict Arnold. What immediately comes to mind? Why? Because every American child is taught early in school to revile Benedict Arnold for betraying the United States during the American Revolution, although later, as adults, we may no longer remember what specifically it was that he did. For the record, Arnold was an outstanding military officer, who became embittered over his perceived mistreatment by the Continental Congress, and decided to switch sides. In 1780, he arranged to have himself put in command of the American fort at West Point, which he then planned to surrender to the British. But the plot was revealed before it could be carried out.

And, although Arnold managed to escape and fled to England, his British co-conspirator, whose capture led to the discovery of the plot, was executed. Perhaps it is because he was never brought to justice that Arnold's name endures in American history as the definition of treason.

The Pentagon in 1962, judged Kennedy's actions to be no different from Arnold. From their point of view, we were at war with the communists, and with the help of his appeasing-father's money, JFK had managed to get himself elected President of the United States, and was now systematically surrendering it to the enemy. They believed that they had to put a stop to it, and they would make sure the traitor would not escape this time. This motive is much simpler and had universal appeal; they could recruit whomever they needed if they could convince them that the President had committed treason. Most people would be willing to risk their lives if they thought it meant the survival of their country.

There is an oft-stated premise put forth by believers of the Warren Commission, that if there was a conspiracy then someone would have talked by now, supposedly out of some feeling of guilt or remorse, and they point to the absence of such a confession in this case as prima fascia evidence that there was no conspiracy. But, guilt or remorse arises from a conscious awareness of wrongdoing. In this case, however, there is no guilt or remorse; the mindset is, rather, quite the opposite. The participants in this little piece of American history consider themselves as having been called upon to carry out a unique patriotic duty. They believed that they had not committed murder; they were convinced that they had executed a traitor, and helped save their country from falling to the communists. As Kennedy himself predicted when he pondered the military coup in the plot of *Seven Days in May*, "the military would feel that it was their patriotic obligation to preserve the nation." And all of them would take a secret like that to their graves.

Dallas

Perhaps tonight I should go to the theater.

JFK to Dave Powers, October 28, 1962
After the resolution of the Cuban Missile Crisis.

Since we do not know all the details of this plot, the tendency has been to view the events surrounding the assassination as though everything that happened that day was how it was planned. But, did all of it go according to plan? There is one aspect that immediately seemed highly dubious in this regard; and that was the arrest and subsequent murder of Lee Oswald. As a television reporter at Dallas police headquarters told viewers just after Oswald's death:

> About the only thing that is clear at this point is that there is not a single police officer in this building who believes that Jack Ruby killed Lee Oswald out of patriotic fervor . . . it was for one reason only, and that was to seal his lips. [88]

For the sake of argument, put yourself in the place of the plotters, as they conspired to kill the President, and, with some common sense reasoning, consider these three issues:

First, out of all possible persons to select as the patsy, why would they choose Oswald, an intelligence agent who had been sent to the Soviet Union as a false defector, and then when he returned was made to appear pro-Castro in the role of the Chairman of a fictitious chapter of the *Fair Play for Cuba Committee*? If, for instance, the only reason for getting rid of JFK was so they could prosecute a war in Vietnam, why not pick someone relatively innocuous who, just for the sake of argument, could be made to appear to hate Kennedy for something else, such as his civil rights policies? They could have likewise directed blame away from themselves and onto that other 'deranged' individual, and would have still been able to have their way in Vietnam. The only reason for pointing the blame at Russia and Cuba would be because that is exactly where they intended it to go.

Secondly, could it have been that having Oswald arrested was the original plan? The FBI taped racketeer Joseph Milteer discussing a plot to assassinate the President in Miami. Describing the plan to shoot the President with a high-powered rifle from a tall building, Milteer says, 'they'll pick up a patsy to throw off the public.' This would lead one to believe that having the patsy arrested was part of the plan. Yet when the assassination actually takes place in Dallas, the conspirators go to a great deal of trouble and exposure-risk to kill the patsy after he is picked up and is guarded by police. The logical conclusion to draw is that the plotters had to have planned to terminate the patsy all along.

And finally, since their intent was to terminate the fall guy, would the conspirators have actually planned for him to just wander off unattended, and then hope he is apprehended, and wait until he is in police custody to try to get him? One would think it would be important to monitor his whereabouts and know where he is at all times during the operation. And would it not have made more sense, and risked less chance of being discovered, to take out the scapegoat as he made his escape, or while 'resisting arrest,' before he had a chance to talk, rather than inside the police station? Numerous authors have suggested that eliminating Oswald was likely J. D. Tippit's assignment. The murder of Officer Tippit has been dubbed the 'Rosetta Stone' of the JFK assassination. This may be true, but not for the reason it was given that title.[89]

Shortly after the President was shot, Tippit was patrolling the Oak Cliff section of Dallas. This area was four miles away from his normal patrol area, but coincidently was the exact part of town where Oswald rented a room. Earlene Roberts, the housekeeper, testified that on November 22, Oswald came back to his room at approximately 1:00 PM, and was inside changing, when a police squad car stopped in front of the rooming house and tapped the horn twice, "as if it were some kind of signal." The car then slowly rolled away. Oswald hurriedly left just afterward, wearing a different shirt and jacket, and carrying his .38 caliber revolver. According to Dallas Police records, the only one of their cars confirmed to be in Oak Cliff at that time was that of Officer J. D. Tippit.

Tippit's actions[90] just before he was murdered give all indications of a man desperately looking for someone, but apparently not as part of his official police business. He was seen sitting in his police car at a Good Luck Oil Company (GLOCO) gas station watching the cars as they drove away from downtown Dallas towards Oak Cliff, across the Houston Street Viaduct, which spans the Trinity River. Tippit suddenly left the gas station and drove away at high speed. Curiously, when the dispatcher asked for his location, he reported himself to be at a different intersection several blocks away. Cab driver William Whaley, who dropped Oswald off near his rooming house, said that on his way there, he had crossed the Houston Street Viaduct, at about the same time Tippit was reported to have been at the gas station.

Tippit was next seen hurriedly entering the *Top Ten Record Shop*, where he asked the clerk to use the phone, forcing his way past customers as he rushed to get to it. He dialed a number but did not say anything, leading the clerk to believe that whomever he was calling did not answer. And it was evidently not a busy signal since he let the phone ring long enough for a number of rings before hanging up. The clerk said he rushed out of the store looking "*upset or worried about something*" and sped away in his police car.

Shortly after this, a Dallas Police Officer stopped a car driven by insurance agent James Andrews, who was travelling west on 10th street. The Officer veered in front of him to cut him off, then jumped out of his squad car and motioned for him not to move. He ran over to Andrews' vehicle and looked into the front and back seats, but completely ignored the driver. The Officer, who Andrews remarked, "seemed to be very upset and agitated and was acting wild" got back in his car and left without saying a word. Andrews, bewildered by the policeman's behavior, made sure to note his nameplate. It read 'Tippit.'

Witnesses say they saw Tippit's car traveling very slowly on 10th street a few moments later. For reasons that will forever be unknown, he stopped his squad car near 10th and Patton to talk to someone on the sidewalk. Some witnesses say it was one, while others report it was a pair of pedestrians that Tippit stopped that day. The man the officer addressed leaned on the passenger side door to talk to him through the open window. During the course of their conversation, the patrolman got out of his car, and was walking around to the front of it, when the individual he was speaking with inexplicably pulled out a gun and shot him three times in the chest. The assailant then stepped into the street, leaned over the fallen officer, and fired a fourth shot, point-blank, into his right temple. Thirty-nine year old Police Officer J. D. Tippit died on the spot, at approximately 1:10PM. His killer(s) escaped on foot. A wallet with identifications for 'Lee Harvey Oswald' and 'Alek Hidell' was found at the scene of the policeman's murder. However, this was a problem, because Oswald still had his real wallet in his pants pocket that had IDs with the same names.

Oswald was likely followed when he left the book depository, however, he must have sensed something had gone awry. Whatever he was told, events were not going according to plan, and he may have even realized that it was him that they were after. His circuitous route back to his rooming house on foot, by bus, and by cab, which included some random direction changes, could well have been evasive maneuvers to shake anyone who he thought might be tailing him. If so, it worked. We can never know what specifically it was that he did differently, but Oswald must have done something to elude the trackers, and in so doing avoided a rendezvous with Tippit. The police officer's frantic search ensued when he realized that he had not completed his task, and he was summarily executed because of this failure. As the House Select Committee on Assassinations, in discussing the murderer's fourth shot concluded:

> This action, which is often encountered in gangland murders and is commonly described as a coup de grace, is *more indicative of an execution* than an act

of defense intended to allow escape or prevent apprehension.[91] [Emphasis added]

Because Tippit failed his assignment, Oswald was able to make his way to the Texas Theater, located just one block away from *The Top Ten Record Shop,* where the slain officer tried to make a phone call only minutes before. Once inside the sparsely filled movie house, Oswald exhibited strange behavior by changing his seat several times. He would choose a person sitting alone and sit directly next to them, but after a few moments would get up and move to another, as though he was searching for a contact he expected to be there. Soon a contingent of police arrived and, after a brief scuffle, Oswald was apprehended, alive. And, as he was taken out, he shouted, "I am not resisting arrest! I am not resisting arrest!" It is notably peculiar that prior to that arrest, Oswald was described as "nervous and fearful," however, after being placed in the police car outside the theater, his demeanor completely reversed. Atypically, it was only after he was in police custody that he calmed down.

When considering if it would have mattered if Oswald had been killed before he could be arrested, the thinking has generally tended toward the belief that it would not have made much difference. The reasoning goes that LBJ would have responded the same way by squashing any discussion of conspiracy, and would still have appointed the Warren Commission, so we would have arrived at the same result. But imagine if a Policeman had confronted Oswald on some street in Oak Cliff, and shot him when he 'resisted arrest.' What then? We would not have any of his now familiar statements as he was led through the police station. We would never have heard, "I didn't do it . . . I didn't shoot anyone, no sir. I'm only a patsy." Gone also would be his denials of the backyard photographs, the purchase of the rifle, the use of various aliases, and all the rest.

On the contrary, Oswald's murder on Sunday morning instead of Friday afternoon made a very crucial difference. By way of comparison, consider what happened thirty-eight years later in the aftermath of the September 11 attacks. On September 12, Mohamed Atta and 18 other suicidal hijackers are identified; Atta's suitcase, found at Logan airport, contained a video on flying airliners, a fuel consumption calculator and a copy of the Koran. Shortly thereafter, it was discovered that they had attended flight schools in the U.S., but did not want to learn how to takeoff or land, they had ties to Al-Qaeda and to Osama Bin Laden. And where did all of that lead?

So now, forget for the moment that you ever saw or heard Lee Oswald in police custody that weekend. Imagine if, on that Friday afternoon, the President is murdered and the escaping assassin is killed in a shoot-out with a Dallas Policeman. It is soon discovered that the gunman was an ex-marine who defected to Russia and returned to the U.S. three years later, married to the niece of a KGB Colonel. There is evidence that he used a false name to purchase the rifle used to kill JFK. There are pictures of the assassin in his backyard brandishing that same rifle, displaying communist newspapers, and the pistol pictured in the holster around his waist is the same one he used when he made his last stand. This would be shortly followed with revelations of his recent trip to Mexico City, where he tried to meet with the KGB head of assassinations, and where he also requested a visa to return to the Soviet Union, via Cuba. The obvious conclusion would have been that the communists were behind the assassination. And where would all of that have led?

Eleven months prior to Dallas, the President held a meeting over the Christmas holidays with the Joint Chiefs of Staff in Palm Beach Florida, primarily to discuss the defense budget for 1964. This meeting occurred only a few weeks after the missile crisis, when the Chiefs were still incensed at the President for his failure to authorize the Cuban invasion. Near the end of the meeting, after Admiral Anderson made passing reference to the recent "Cuban situation," JFK followed on with a clumsily transparent attempt to placate the military's anger, as he began discussing plans for future action against Cuba: He assured them that,

> . . . although we feel that the present Cuban situation is dormant, we must assume that someday we may have to go into Cuba, and when it happens, we must be prepared to do it as quickly as possible, with a minimum

of destruction . . . . The President pointed out that he felt
this was a possibility in the next few years whether he was
president or not, and that they had to plan for this.[92]

Surely, this time the Chiefs must have been convinced they were
being patronized. They undoubtedly wondered how Kennedy could
be seriously discussing plans for a future invasion of Cuba when he
had just reneged on the golden opportunity to do precisely that. After
their numerous futile attempts to concoct a pretext for an invasion,
the Soviets had given them their perfect justification. They could not
have asked for a better chance. World opinion was on their side; the
weapons were ready; and the troops were boarding ships. And at the
last moment, they believed he chickened out. They probably asked
themselves; just whom did he think he was fooling here? They had
to face facts; in spite of what he was now saying, John Kennedy was
never going to invade Cuba. He had gone so far as to assure the Soviet
Union and the world that he would not.

Therefore, they see no other choice except to do exactly as he said.
And they prepare to do it as quickly as possible; however, they opt
for the latter case, when he was no longer president, because the first
step of this plan will be his extremely violent and public execution. A
pre-arranged patsy will take the blame, who, as he attempts to flee,
will be killed by a policeman when he 'resists arrest.' Next, evidence
will be 'discovered' that the accused gunman was a communist agent
sent by Russia and Cuba to assassinate the President. Two hundred
million Americans will absolutely howl for vengeance. A decisive
retaliatory attack on Cuba will quickly follow. But, you may ask, what
about that no-invasion pledge? Well, on closer examination one finds
that that was strictly a personal commitment by JFK. It was certainly
never sanctioned by the military, and, in fact, it was never actually
formalized by the President either. In any event, the point would
be moot; because the pledge would then be void, since the person
who made it had been murdered by the people he made it to. And a
year after the Missile Crisis, an invasion of Cuba was going to be a
cakewalk, because the missiles were gone, as were the IL-28 bombers,
along with the Soviet technicians. When the Russians respond, the
U.S. military would finally be able to launch the pre-emptive strike

they had been planning for all these years. It was going to be the ultimate false-flag operation, Lemnitzer's magnum opus.

And notice the timing. It was late 1963, and, as suggested by the Net Evaluation Subcommittee in 1961, it was the optimum time for *". . . a surprise attack preceded by a period of heightened tensions."* Tensions resulting from the assassination of the President of the United States by an agent of a communist country.

Authors Noel Twyman in *Bloody Treason,* and James Douglass in *JFK and The Unspeakable,* both consider this possibility. Mr. Twyman dismisses it as too far-fetched, and although Mr. Douglass examines it in more detail, he finally concludes that it did not work because by then he believes that JFK had persuaded the Chiefs that a pre-emptive strike was not winnable, and that in the end, Johnson diverted attention away from the Soviets. In each case, the author has made this connection, but did not have the key piece of the puzzle— why the military would want to kill their own president just to start a war. But, given its purpose of undoing the 'treason' that they believe JFK committed in the Cuban settlement, it all becomes crystal clear.[93] According to an NSA Intelligence Report dated November 27, 1963, the first person to realize that the assassination was intended as a pretext to attack Cuba was Fidel Castro himself:

> . . . [Oswald's background] caused Castro to wonder whether the assassin was not the mere instrument of a monstrous plot of the American militarists who, by eliminating Kennedy, would put Johnson in a position from which there would be only one way out; to drain off anti-Cuba hysteria by an action of declared war. [94]

The same NSA communication also reports that Castro was also aware of the 'heightened tensions' expected at the end of 1963:

> In fact, it is the general opinion in [redacted] circles that Castro feared that the assassination would be the spring which would unleash passions and violent and blind hysteria of the American people against Cuba and Russia

and provide the excuse, which up to now was lacking to justify internationally an invasion of Cuba. *There is talk again about the coincidence of rumors concerning a crisis at the end of the year.* [Emphasis added]

Although each of the Chiefs wanted to remove the President, which of them would have taken the initiative to actually organize and carry out this plot? Who was what Noel Twyman termed the assassination's "mastermind?" Consider the answers to these questions:

- Who accused the President of cowardice during the Bay of Pigs, and talked about removing him from office then?
- Who repeatedly tried to provoke the U.S.S.R. into starting a war during the Cuban Missile Crisis?
- Who accused JFK of appeasement during that crisis, the person most enraged by its outcome, and who pronounced the Cuban settlement to be 'the worst defeat in our history'?
- Who believed that nuclear war with the Russians was inevitable, so we should get it over with now while we have the advantage, and had been trying to start that war since the first Eisenhower administration?
- Who demonstrated time and again that he was willing to take matters into his own hands and do whatever *he* believed necessary to protect his country?

Based on the preponderance of evidence, the logical answer is one person, and one person only. And that person is Four-Star General Curtis E. LeMay, Chief of Staff, United States Air Force. In the autobiography he wrote just two years after the President's murder, LeMay explained why he was obligated to kill.

It was because I was part of a primitive world where men still had to kill in order to avoid being killed, or in order to avoid having their beloved Nation stricken and emasculated.

Evidently, the latter was the Defendant's justification for adding JFK to his astoundingly long list. He was just one more.

Cryptogram

In fact, the firing squad left a record, albeit unintentionally, revealing whom it was that sent them. A year and a day after Kennedy officially ended the naval quarantine, a Cuban man stands on the sidewalk of a Dallas street waiting for the President's motorcade to pass by. He is standing near a second man in a sport coat who, on this perfectly sunny day, is the only person in Dealey Plaza carrying an umbrella. The President's limousine makes the hard left turn onto Elm Street, and then slows perceptibly as it approaches them. The man in the sport coat has now opened the iconic LARGE BLACK UMBRELLA. When the President's car gets close, he pumps it up and down conspicuously to make sure that Kennedy notices. At the same time, his Cuban associate is likewise drawing attention as he stands nearest the street, prominently waving with his right hand raised high over his head. The two are completely oblivious to the unmistakable sound of gunfire that suddenly erupts in volleys from the surrounding plaza. But then, these men were not ordinary spectators; they were part of what happened that day. Their assignment was to deliver a final message to John F. Kennedy.[95] They were there to let the President know *why* this was about to be the last few seconds of his life. In tandem, they are heralding, "Ap*peasement—Cuba.*" Whether or not JFK understood that message is, of course, unknowable. But, because these men happened to be within range of Abraham Zapruder's viewfinder, the Defendants' cold-blooded sendoff has been preserved for the ages.

In the chaos after the shooting, the second man closes his umbrella and the pair calmly sit down together on the curb and chat, while most others run about frantically. The Cuban briefly speaks into a poorly concealed two-way radio and, after a few minutes, the two men get up and very nonchalantly walk away in opposite directions.[96]

The first part of the plan had been accomplished; JFK was out of the way. But, because Lee Harvey Oswald managed to survive that Friday afternoon, the other parts of the plan: undoing the Cuban settlement, getting rid of Castro, and forcing a showdown with Khrushchev, all came to naught.

Alibi

Curtis LeMay was reportedly on a hunting trip in upstate Michigan when the President's execution was carried out in Dallas. According to his biography, LeMay claimed that he was at a place so remote, that he was just able to make it back to Washington in time for the funeral[97]. But, salvaged records from Andrews Air Force Base for that day prove otherwise. The Log Book shows that less than an hour after the assassination, LeMay ordered an Air Force C-140 to pick him up at Wiarton, a Canadian Air Force base north of Toronto[98]. Conveniently, the General was out of the country when the shooting took place. After all, if JFK had somehow survived, a real investigation would lead directly back to him. Once news of the President's death was broadcast, it was safe for him to come back.

Furthermore, recently discovered recordings[99] show that Air Force One received messages from LeMay, relayed through the White House situation room as both planes were enroute to Washington. The Chief of Staff wanted confirmation that the late President's body was on board the plane, and then machinated the autopsy arrangements. And, contrary to his assertions, LeMay actually arrived back in Washington an hour before Air Force One touched down. However, he did not land at Andrews, as ordered by the Secretary of the Air Force, who wanted him to be there to greet the Presidents' plane. He landed at Washington National airport instead.

Washington National is closer to Bethesda Naval Hospital, which is exactly where technicians assisting at the President's autopsy saw the Defendant late that Friday night, along with many other members of the Pentagon's top brass.[100] He coolly smoked one of his trademark cigars as they all watched the grisly proceedings from the packed gallery in Bethesda's morgue. It was a standing-room-only event. It seems more than a little odd that so many of the nation's top military officers would be in attendance. But, they were there to make sure that the evidence showed only shots from behind the President. They manipulated and/or falsified every aspect of the post mortem to make sure of it, and then swore all subordinate witnesses to secrecy, under threat of court martial.

Aftershock

Johnson Press Secretary Bill Moyers told James Galbraith Jr. that on Air Force One on the way home from Dallas that, for a long time, LBJ just stared out the window. Moyers asked him what he was concerned about. LBJ responded that he was wondering if the missiles had started flying. Moyers understood this to mean that Johnson expected the military to be preparing to launch a nuclear first strike against the Soviet Union[101]. By the time LBJ said this, he was informed that the patsy accused of committing the assassination was an ex-marine turned pro-Cuban Soviet communist. Johnson also knew what the military's nuclear war plans were; after all, the Burris Memorandum was written for him. Perhaps he just figured out the parts of the plot of which he had not been informed.

Nervous leaders in Moscow and Havana were wondering the exact same thing. Nikita Khrushchev and Fidel Castro each believed that they would be blamed for the President's death. The Soviet Union and Cuba both quietly went on military alert on the evening of November 22. Large numbers of troops were deployed around Havana and the northern coast of Cuba in anticipation of an attack from the United States.[102]

During the week following the assassination, the new president effectively rescinded JFK's plan for withdrawing American advisors from Vietnam. Then, pre-empting likely investigations by the Dallas Police Department, the State of Texas, the Department of Justice, and the United States Congress, LBJ appointed a Presidential Commission to investigate his predecessor's death; a commission that he controlled. He used the threat of nuclear war to cajole Chief Justice Earl Warren to lead it, as well as to pressure a few of the more reluctant candidates to accept the assignment. As one of the Committee's members Johnson chose CIA's ex-Director Allen Dulles, General Lansdale's patron, who JFK had fired after the Bay of Pigs fiasco. Johnson also ordered his good friend, FBI Director J. Edgar Hoover, to seize all evidence in the case. The foxes guarded the henhouse. After ten months of investigation, to almost no one's surprise, the Warren Commission certified that Lee Harvey Oswald had singlehandedly assassinated President John F. Kennedy and murdered Dallas Police Officer J. D. Tippit, and that there was no larger conspiracy, foreign or domestic. The cover-up complete, and wrapped in a twenty-six volume bow.

~

The Defendants and their accomplices have all since left this earth, and can no longer stand trial for the President's murder. In the name of saving their country from 'communism,' they perverted the government they sought to preserve, just as JFK warned, "only God knows just what segment of democracy they would be defending if they overthrew the elected establishment." If we are ever going to get our government back, we need to know the truth about what happened to it in the late fall of 1963. It is for this purpose that this Case is respectfully submitted to the verdict of history.

The Prosecution rests.

Epilogue

<u>Fidel Alejandro Castro Ruz</u> was having lunch with French journalist Jean Daniel on November 22, 1963. Daniel had come to Havana with a message from JFK. The President would consider rapprochement with Cuba if they removed all Soviet forces, ended subversion in the western hemisphere, and remained unaligned in the Cold War. Castro was keenly interested, and as the two men discussed a response for Daniel to convey to Washington, they received news of the President's murder. Castro immediately stood up, blurting out, "Everything has changed!" The Cuban leader's subsequent attempts to continue this discussion with the next administration were ignored.

Afterward, Castro returned to the repressive tactics he employed since the revolution. He utilized American threats and harassment as a means to consolidate power and to crush internal dissent. Maintaining this siege mentality sustained Fidel in office through the next eight American presidents. Cuba was economically supported by the Soviet Union until its own demise in 1991. Since then Cuba has just managed to make do in the face of the economic embargo that the U.S. imposed in 1962, and maintains to this day.

Castro far outlasted every one of his cold war contemporaries. But, after suffering a near-fatal intestinal infection in early 2006, Fidel turned over the Cuban presidency to his brother Raúl. In April 2011, exactly fifty years since officially turning to socialism, the frail 84-year-old dictator officially resigned as the First Secretary of the Communist Party of Cuba.

Economic reforms have recently been proposed which would bring major changes to the island nation. For the first time in five decades, Cubans may soon be able to own property and establish their own businesses. Indications are that communism in Cuba will likely end with Fidel. Not with a bang but a whimper.

Nikita Sergeyevich Khrushchev never did believe the U.S. government's official version of the Kennedy assassination. The Soviet Premier's early suspicions were reinforced when the KGB told him that they believed the murder was "organized by a circle of reactionary monopolists in league with pro-fascist groups in the U.S."[103] Then, in May 1964, his old friend, Washington columnist Drew Pearson and his wife visited with Mr. and Mrs. Khrushchev in Moscow. The two women were mutual friends of the wife of Supreme Court Chief Justice Earl Warren, so when the conversation inevitably turned to the Commission's ongoing investigation, the Soviet Premier asked the reporter to tell him what *really* happened in Dallas. Pearson answered that he believed that the initial assertions were correct, that Oswald was the lone assassin; but Khrushchev refused to accept it. The Pearsons' further efforts to defend the official story were met with 'tolerant smiles' from the Soviet leader and his wife. "The Khrushchevs remained convinced that the official version of the assassination story was false." [104]

Yet, on some level, Khrushchev must have realized who was really behind the assassination, since, during what the Russians refer to as the 'Caribbean Crisis,' the Soviet leader faced the exact same pressures from the military in Moscow that his American counterpart faced from the military in Washington:

> Khrushchev told Norm Cousins in 1963, "When I asked the military advisers if they could assure me that holding fast would not result in the deaths of five-hundred million human beings, they looked at me as though I was out of my mind or, what was worse, a *traitor*. The biggest tragedy, as they saw it, was not that our country might be devastated and everything lost, but that the Chinese or the Albanians would accuse us of *appeasement* or weakness."[105] [Emphasis added]

Confronted with the grim alternatives, Khrushchev, in the end, made the same choice that Kennedy did, as he later mused:

> What good would it have done me in the last hour of my life
> to know that though our great nation and the United States
> were in complete ruins, the national honor of the Soviet
> Union was intact?[106]

However, the Soviet Premier would not pay as high a price for his decision as the American President had to pay for his. On his return from an extended vacation in October 1964, Khrushchev was ousted in a Kremlin coup orchestrated by his replacement, Leonoid Bhreshnev. Counted amongst the justifications for his removal was his responsibility for risking nuclear war by installing Soviet missiles in Cuba. At the end of this great misadventure, the international prestige of the United States had significantly increased at the expense of the Soviet Union's, which had suffered when they were forced to withdraw their missiles, troops, and aircraft. The American non-invasion pledge concluding the crisis was not worth the price of obtaining it. Khrushchev had risked the total annihilation of their Homeland, in exchange for the verbal pledge of a capitalist Statesman, just to protect a small, remote satellite nation. And, just one year after that pledge was made; the Statesman who made it was gone.

Afterward, Khrushchev became a 'non-person,' condemned to spend the remainder of his life under the 'protection' of security guards in the prison of his own residence. He descended into a deep depression as his movements, his few visitors and his conversations came under constant surveillance. In 1966, Khrushchev began to record his memoirs on audio tape, fully aware that the KGB was listening to every word. Two years into the project, Khrushchev was ordered to turn over the recordings, but he refused. The KGB eventually confiscated the tapes, but not before his son, Sergei, smuggled a copy to the West, where they were published in 1970 under the title, "*Khrushchev Remembers.*" Predictably, the Soviet Union promptly denounced them as fraud. Khrushchev died of a heart attack at the age of 77, on September 11, 1971. The Soviet government denied him a traditional state funeral and the honor of interment in the Kremlin Wall.

Lyndon Bains Johnson finished Kennedy's term and was then elected to his own in 1964. During his campaign against Republican Barry Goldwater, Johnson successfully painted himself as the peace candidate and his opponent as a warmonger.[107] But, a few months before the election, Johnson used the *Gulf of Tonkin Incident*[108] as a pretext to order a U.S. attack on North Vietnam. It was his first overt step into a conflict that would quickly lead to his deployment of U.S. combat troops. Before it was over, that war would claim the lives of three million, four hundred thousand Vietnamese, in addition to fifty-eight thousand Americans.

And so, the bet Johnson placed in accepting the vice presidential position paid off. At the age of 55, he finally got the job he had coveted all his life. But, after a little more than one term, he had all he could stomach. The more he escalated the war in Vietnam, the more unpopular it became, and the louder rose the chorus of anti-war demonstrators chanting slogans such as, "HEY! HEY! L-B-J!—HOW MANY KIDS DID YOU KILL TODAY?" According to Lady Byrd Johnson, in the latter years of his presidency, Lyndon was drinking heavily, and hardly sleeping at night, frequently roaming the White House halls and checking the latest casualty figures instead. In addition to the heavy personal toll, the war began to have major political consequences. His public support started to fall off sharply in early 1968 after the North launched a major offensive throughout the South on the first day of the Vietnamese Tết holiday. That spring, several members of his own party entered the primary race to challenge him for the Democratic nomination. But Johnson had had enough. He unexpectedly concluded a nationally televised address in the final hours of March with the announcement that he would not seek, nor would he accept, the nomination of his party for another term as America's president. The following January 20th, LBJ relinquished to his successor the reins of power he had struggled so long and hard to attain, and then withdrew to his Texas ranch.

In retirement, he lived like a hermit, let his hair grow long, and sank further into the depression that began during his final years in office. His mental state continued to erode as his depression became despair, and finally paranoia, obsessively talking of conspiracies in which 'THEY' were out to get him.[109] To sleep at night he often needed someone he trusted sitting outside his bedroom door. [110] His lawyers brought psychiatrists to the ranch for an evaluation, but whatever Johnson told them was never revealed.[111] LBJ suffered a heart attack and died, alone in his room, on January 22, 1973, at the comparatively young age of 64. In an ironic twist of fate, the next day 37th President Richard Nixon appeared on national television to announce the signing of the Paris Peace Accords, achieving "peace with honor" and bringing an end to American involvement in the war in Vietnam.

Robert Francis Kennedy immediately suspected who was actually behind his brother's murder; but for the sake of appearances, gave lip service to the lone-nut fable. Only a week after the assassination, he sent a message to Khrushchev through a back channel between family friend Bill Walton and Georgi Bolshakov. The first part of the message was that both Robert and Jacqueline Kennedy believed that the President had been killed by a domestic right-wing conspiracy.[112] The second part of the message was that the cooling of US-Soviet relations, expected to occur in the upcoming Johnson administration, would not be permanent. RFK intended to bide his time and run for Governor of Massachusetts in order to build sufficient political capital for a later run for president. When he attained the White House, he would continue his brother's efforts at détente.[113]

Instead, nine months after his brother's funeral, he left the Justice Department to run as the Democratic candidate in the 1964 U.S. Senate race in New York. He won the seat, despite accusations from his Republican opponent that the Massachusetts native was a 'carpetbagger.' In mid-March 1968, RFK joined the growing opposition to LBJ's re-nomination when he announced his candidacy for the presidency, on the exact same spot where his brother had announced his eight years earlier. It was shortly after his entry into the race that Johnson threw in the towel.

Robert Kennedy was shot point-blank in the back of the head on June 5th, supposedly by a man facing him across the room. The 42-year-old Senator was on his way out of the hotel where he had just delivered his victory speech on winning the California presidential primary, which significantly improved his chances of receiving the Democratic nomination. He died the next day. Why was Bobby killed? Perhaps it was because RFK had been an integral part of the 'treasonous' Cuban settlement. But, the more pressing imperative was that, if elected, there was little doubt he would re-open the investigation of his brother's murder.

<u>Robert Strange McNamara</u> maintained his position as Secretary of Defense in the Johnson administration. He had been for the war in Vietnam in 1961, for withdrawal in 1963, and then for the war again in 1964. In the 2004 Errol Morris documentary, *The Fog Of War: Eleven Lessons From The Life Of Robert S. McNamara*, the former Defense Secretary confirms that the Kennedy administration planned to bring all American advisors home from Vietnam by 1965. "But-", he explains, "-there was a coup," then, almost as an afterthought adds, "in South Vietnam,"—presumably to clarify exactly to which coup he was referring.

From 1964 through 1967, McNamara applied the full weight of his considerable energies into the prosecution of the ever-widening war in Vietnam. He became so thoroughly immersed in the effort that many began to refer to Vietnam as 'McNamara's War', a moniker that, at the time, he was proud of. He was forced out by Johnson in early 1968 after sending the 36th President a memorandum recommending de-escalation of the war and a negotiated withdrawal from Vietnam. As a sop, Johnson awarded him the Medal of Freedom, and then sent him off to head the World Bank. McNamara eventually came to believe that the war in Vietnam was a mistake.

In 1995, he participated in a conference in Vietnam to discuss the causes and effects of the war with his previous enemies. Nguyen Co Thach, the former Foreign Minister of Vietnam, argued with McNamara, telling the former Secretary that the United States was completely wrong in presuming that the Vietnamese were fighting to advance communism. McNamara, the one-time 'Whiz Kid,' who had always prided himself on his thorough preparation and mastery of the facts on any given topic, relates how, in this case, the Foreign Minister scolded him:

> We were fighting for our independence. You were fighting
> to enslave us. Mr. McNamara, you must never have read a
> history book. If you had, you'd know we weren't pawns of

the Chinese or the Russians. McNamara, didn't you know that? Don't you understand that we have been fighting the Chinese for a thousand years? We were fighting for our independence. And we would fight to the last man. And we were determined to do so. And no amount of bombing, no amount of U.S. pressure would ever have stopped us.[114]

It would seem that this particular *Lesson from the Life of Robert S. McNamara* was learned much too late to benefit the nearly three and a half million lives that were violently cut short because of that war. Conversely, the much longer life of Robert S. McNamara came to a decidedly more tranquil end in the early morning hours of July 6, 2009, as he slept in his Washington D.C. home. He was 93.[115]

Lyman Louis Lemnitzer commanded NATO until his retirement in July 1969. Six years afterward, the 38th President, and former Warren Commissioner, Gerald Ford, appointed the General to serve on the Rockefeller Commission. This latest Presidential Commission was set-up to investigate the myriad reports of illegal CIA activities, certain of which were related to the Kennedy Assassination.

One in particular developed from the public's growing distrust of the Warren Commission findings and the festering calls for a new investigation into the President's murder. Complaints arose after the Zapruder Film was shown to the public for the first time, twelve years after it was recorded. Clearly, the rearward snap of the President's head was evidence of a shot from the front, which the Warren Commission obviously missed.

Lemnitzer produced the Rockefeller Commission's conclusion on this issue with the stupefying rationalization that there could not have been a shot from the front, because there is no evidence of one in the Warren Commission report. Having thus papered over traces of his unfulfilled masterpiece, Lemnitzer slipped back into retirement. In November 1988, at age 89, Lemnitzer, like all old soldiers, just faded away. He is buried in Arlington National Cemetery, in the section adjacent to JFK.

<u>Curtis Emerson LeMay</u> was reappointed as Chief of the Air Force by Johnson for a one-year term, and then put out to pasture in early 1965. Once ensconced in his own presidency, LBJ made sure to close the door behind him. In retirement, LeMay declined several offers to run for political office, but changed his mind in October 1968, when he agreed to be George Wallace's vice presidential running mate on the American Independent ticket. LeMay did this, he told a friend, to help Richard Nixon by drawing votes away from Hubert Humphrey. A televised press conference was arranged to announce his acceptance of the nomination. But, instead of talking about something relevant,— like the campaign—LeMay, to the shock and horror of viewers, launched into a seven-minute screed advocating the use of nuclear weapons in Vietnam. For an encore, he jumped into an argument with his running mate on live TV. After the presidential candidate attempted to downplay his remarks, the General shot back that he meant exactly what he said. A leopard simply cannot change its spots.

Afterward, LeMay became a recluse who rarely left his retirement home near March AFB, California. He passed away peacefully, ironically, at the age of 84, convinced to the bitter end that America had lost the Cold War because JFK passed up the opportunity to invade Cuba and get rid of Castro.

In January 1992, organizers arranged what would be the final conference to re-examine the events of the Cuban Missile Crisis. Among the attendees at this Havana session was Robert McNamara, as well as many of the other surviving participants, including this time, Cuban Premier Fidel Castro.

The singularly horrific revelation from this conference was that, had Kennedy listened to LeMay and approved the General's planned invasion of Cuba in October 1962, it would have certainly unleashed the Armageddon.[116] Because, in addition to the presence of another 30,000 Soviet soldiers that the U.S. was completely unaware of—and, contrary to everything American intelligence believed at the time—there were, in fact, nuclear warheads already in Cuba for 162 ballistic missiles capable of reaching major cities in the United States, plus 90 tactical missiles for use against invading American forces. The Soviet commanders and their Cuban allies had authorization to use these tactical weapons, and Castro stated unequivocally that they would have launched them in the event of a U.S. attack.[117] This news stunned the former Defense Secretary, who instantly recognized how events would have consequently played out: in accordance with SIOP, SAC would have immediately launched a retaliatory strike, triggering a full-scale thermonuclear exchange with the Soviet Union. Of that eventuality, contemporary estimates[118] are that, in the final analysis, nearly one third of the three billion people who then inhabited this small planet, who all breathed the same air, who all cherished their children's futures, would all be mortalities.

It is a half century after the assassination. A large majority of Americans do not believe the official version of events that occurred on that long ago November day. No matter. The United States Government can never, and will never, admit to the real reason for the assassination. The truth is that American military leaders were perfectly willing to risk the lives of a billion men, women, and children, in order to eliminate one man in Cuba. They murdered John Fitzgerald Kennedy because he was not.

Bibliography

Bamford, James. *Body of Secrets: Anatomy of the Ultra-secret National Security Agency: from the Cold War through the Dawn of a New Century*. New York: Doubleday, 2001.

Bird, Kai, and Martin J Sherwin. *American Prometheus:The Triumph and Tragety of J. Robert Oppenheimer*. New York: Alfred A. Knopf, 2005.

Blight, James G, Bruce J. Allyn, and David A. Welch. *Cuba on the Brink: Castro, the Missile Crisis, and the Soviet Collapse*. Lanham, Md: Rowman & Littlefield, 2002.

Blight, James G., Janet M. Lang, and David A. Welch. *Vietnam If Kennedy Had Lived: Virtual JFK*. Lanham, Md: Rowman & Littlefield, 2009.

Brinkley, Douglas. Dean Acheson: the Cold War Years, 1953-71. New Haven: Yale UP, 1992. n.d.

Brugioni, Dino A., and Robert F. McCort. *Eyeball to Eyeball: the inside Story of the Cuban Missile Crisis*. New York: Random House, 1991.

Carroll, James. *House of War: the Pentagon and the Disastrous Rise of American Power*. Boston: Houghton Mifflin, 2006.

Chang, Laurence, and Peter Kornbluh. *The Cuban Missile Crisis, 1962: a National Security Archive Documents Reader*. New York: New, 1992.

Coffey, Thomas M. *Iron Eagle: The Turbulent Life of General Curtis LeMay*. New York: Crown Publishing, 1986.

Dallek, Robert. *An Unfinished Life: John F. Kennedy, 1917-1963*. Boston: Brown and Little, 2003.

Douglass, James W. *JFK and the Unspeakable: Why He Died and Why It Matters*. Maryknoll, N.Y.: Orbis, 2008.

Drenas, William M. "Car #10 Where Are You?" *The Kennedy Assassination*. October 1998. <http://mcadams.posc.mu.edu/car10. htm> (accessed March 12, 2011).

Eden, Lynn. *Whole World on Fire: Organizations, Knowledge, and Nuclear Weapons Devastation*. Ithaca, N.Y.: Cornell UP, 2004.

Ellsberg, Daniel. *Secrets: A Memoir of Vietnam and the Pentagon Papers*. New York: Viking, 2002.

Escalante, Font Fabián. *JFK : the Cuba Files: The Untold Story of the Plot to Kill Kennedy*. Melbourne: Ocean, 2005.

Faber, David. *Munich, 1938: Appeasement and World War II*. New York: Simon & Schuster, 2008.

Fetzer, James H. *Assassination Science: Experts Speak out on the Death of JFK*. Chicago: Catfeet, 1998.

_____. *Murder in Dealey Plaza: What We Know Now That We Didn't Know Then about the Death of JFK*. Chicago: Catfeet, 2000.

_____. *The Great Zapruder Film Hoax: Deceit and Deception in the Death of JFK*. Chicago: Catfeet, 2003.

Fonzi, Gaeton. *The Last Investigation*. New York: Thunder's Mouth, 1993.

Freed, Donald, and Mark Lane. *Executive Action: Assassination of a Head of State*. New York: Dell Pub, 1973.

Fursenko, A. A., and Timothy J. Naftali. *One Hell of a Gamble: Khrushchev, Castro, and Kennedy, 1958-1964*. New York: Norton, 1997.

Gaither, H. Rowan, et. al. *Deterrence & Survival in the Nuclear Age*. A.K.A. 'The Gaither Report', Washington: Office of Defense Mobilization, November 7, 1957.

Garrison, Jim. *A Heritage of Stone*. New York: Berkley Pub., 1975.

Garrison, Jim. *On the Trail of the Assassins*. New York: Warner, 1991.

Goldstein, Gordon M. *Lessons in Disaster: McGeorge Bundy and the Path to War in Vietnam*. New York: Henry Holt and Times , 2009.

Goldwater, Barry Morris. *Why Not Victory?* NewYork: Macfadden-Bartell Corporation, 1962.

Goodwin, Doris Kearns. *Lyndon Johnson and the American Dream*. New York : St. Martin's, 1991.

Groden, Robert J. *The Killing of a President: the Complete Photographic Record of the JFK Assassination, The Conspiracy and the Cover-up*. New York: Viking Studio, 1993.

Groden, Robert J., and Harrison Edward Livingstone. *High Treason: the Assassination of President John F. Kennedy : What Really Happened*. New York: Conservatory, 1989.

Hershberg, Jim. "Anatomy of a controversy: Anatoly F. Dobrynin's Meeting with Robert F. Kennedy Saturday 27 October, 1962." *The Cold War International History Project Bulletin—Issue 5—Spring*, 1995: 80.

Horne, Douglas P. *Inside the Assassination Records Review Board: The U.S. Government's Final Attempt to Reconcile the Conflicting Medical Evidence in the Assassination of JFK*. Falls Church, VA: D. P. Horne, 2009.

Hurt, Henry. *Reasonable Doubt: An Investigation into the Assassination of John F. Kennedy.* New York: Holt, Rinehart, and Winston, 1985.

Kahn, Herman. *On Thermonuclear War.* New Brunswick: Transaction Publishers, 2007.

Kaplan, Fred M. *The Wizards of Armageddon.* Stanford, California: Stanford UP, 1991.

Khrushchev, Nikita Sergeevich, Edward Crankshaw, and Strobe Talbott. *Khrushchev Remembers.* Boston: Brown and Little, 1970.

Klaber, William, and Philip Melanson. *Shadow Play: The Murder of Robert F. Kennedy, the Trial of Sirhan Sirhan, and the Failure of American Justice.* New York: St. Martin's, 1997.

Kohn, Richard H., and Joseph P. Harahan. *Strategic Air Warefare: An Interview with Generals Curtis E. LeMay, Leon W. Johnson, David A. Burchinal, and Jack J. Catton.* Washington, DC: Office of Air Force History, USAF, 1988.

Kornbluh, Peter. *Bay of Pigs Declassified: The Secret CIA Report on the Invasion of Cuba.* New York: New, 1988.

Kozak, Warren. *LeMay: The Life and Wars of General Curtis LeMay.* Washington, D.C.: Regenery Pub., 2009.

Lane, Mark. *Plausible Denial: Was the CIA Involved in the Assassination of JFK?* New York: Thunder's Mouth, 1991.

Law, William Matson. *In the Eye of History: Bethesda Hospital Medical Evidence in the JFK Assassination.* Southlake, TX: JFK Lancer Productions and Publications, 2005.

Lifton, David S. *Best Evidence: Disguise and Deception in the Assassination of John F. Kennedy.* New York: Macmillan, 1980.

Livingstone, Harrison Edward, and Robert J. Groden. *High Treason 2: the Great Cover-up : the Assassination of President John F. Kennedy.* New York: Carroll & Graf, 1992.

Lukacs, John. *George Kennan: A Study of Character.* New Haven, CT: Yale UP, 2009.

Marrs, Jim. *Crossfire: the Plot That Killed Kennedy.* New York: Carroll & Graf, 1989.

McClellan, Barr. *Blood, Money & Power: How LBJ Killed JFK.* New York: Hannover House, 2003.

McDonald, Hugh C, and Geoffrey Bocca. *Appointment in Dallas the Final Solution to the Assassination of JFK.* New York: H. McDonald Pub., 1975.

The Fog of War: Eleven Lessons from The Life of Robert S. McNamara. Directed by Errol Morris. Performed by Robert S. McNamara. 2004.

McNamara, Robert S., and Brian VanDeMark. *In Retrospect: the Tragedy and Lessons of Vietnam.* New York: Vintage, 1996.

Meagher, Sylvia. *Accessories after the Fact: the Warren Commission, the Authorities, and the Report.* New York: Vintage, 1976.

Melanson, Philip H. *Spy Saga: Lee Harvey Oswald and U.S. Intelligence.* New York: Praeger, 1990.

————. *The Robert F. Kennedy Assassination: New Revelations on the Conspiracy and Cover-up, 1968-1991.* New York: Shapolsky, 1991.

Mellen, Joan. *A Farewell to Justice: Jim Garrison, JFK's Assassination, and the Case That Should Have Changed History.* Dulles, VA : Potomac, 2005.

Morrow, Robert D. *First Hand Knowledge: How I Participated in the CIA-Mafia Murder of President Kennedy.* New York: S.P.I., 1992.

Naftali, Timothy, and Philip Zelikow. *The Presidential Recordings John F. Kennedy: The Great Crises II, September-October 1962.* Edited by Philip Zelikow and Ernest May. New York: W. W. Norton & Company, 2001.

Nash, Philip. *The Other Missiles of October: Eisenhower, Kennedy, and the Jupiters, 1957-1963.* Chapel Hill: University of California, 1997.

Newhouse, John. *War and Peace in the Nuclear Age.* New York: Knopf, 1989.

Newman, John M. *JFK and Vietnam: Deception, Intrigue, and the Struggle for Power.* New York: Warner, 1992.

North, Mark. *Act of Treason: The Role of J. Edgar Hoover in the Assassination of President Kennedy.* New York: Carroll & Graf, 1991.

Oglesby, Carl. *The Yankee and Cowboy War: Conspiracies from Dallas to Watergate and beyond.* New York: Berkley Pub, 1977.

————. *Who Killed JFK?* Berkeley, CA: Odonian, 1992.

Perlstein, Rick. *Before the Storm: Barry Goldwater and the Unmaking of the American Concensus.* New York: National , A Member of the Perseus Group, E-Book ed, 2009.

Pfiffer, Jack. "The Official History of the Bay of Pigs Operation." In *Vol. 3: Evolution of CIA's Anti-Castro Policies, 1951-January 1961,* by Jack Pfiffer, CIA Miscellaneous, Box 1. College Park, MD: National Archives JFK Assassination Records Collection, 1992.

Pringle, Peter, and William M. Arkin. *SIOP, the Secret U.S. Plan for Nuclear War.* New York: Norton, 1983.

Prouty, L. Fletcher. *JFK: the CIA, Vietnam, and the Plot to Assassinate John F. Kennedy.* New York: Carol Pub. Group, 1992.

Representatives, The United States House of. *The Final Assassinations Report.* Congressional, New York: Bantam, 1979.

Rhodes, Richard. *Dark Sun: the Making of the Hydrogen Bomb.* New York: Simon & Schuster, 1995.

_____. *The Making of the Atomic Bomb.* New York: Simon & Schuster, 1988.

Roberts, Craig. *Kill Zone: a Sniper Looks at Dealey Plaza.* Tulsa, OK: Consolidated International, 1994.

Sagan, Scott Douglas. "SIOP-62: The Nuclear War Plan Briefing to President Kennedy." *International Security*, 12.1-1987: 22-51.

_____. *The Limits of Safety: Organizations, Accidents, and Nuclear Weapons.* Princeton, N.J.: Princeton UP, 1993.

Scheim, David E. *Contract on America: the Mafia Murder of President John F. Kennedy.* New York: Shapolsky, 1988.

Schlesinger, Arthur M. *A Thousand Days: John F. Kennedy in the White House.* Boston: Houghton Mifflin, 1965.

_____. *Robert Kennedy and His times.* Boston: Houghton Mifflin, 1978.

Scott, Peter Dale. *Deep Politics and the Death of JFK.* Berkeley: University of California, 1996.

Shaw, J. Gary, and Larry Ray Harris. *Cover-Up.* Austin,TX: Collector's Editions, 1992.

Sherwin, Martin J. *A World Destroyed: Hiroshima and Its Legacies.* Stanford, California: Stanford UP, 2003.

Sloan, Bill,, and Jean Hill. *JFK: the Last Dissenting Witness*. Gretna, LA: Pelican Pub, 1992.

Talbot, David. *Brothers: the Hidden History of the Kennedy Years*. New York: Free, 2008.

Thompson, Josiah. *Six Seconds in Dallas*. New York: Berkley Pub., 1976.

Twyman, Noel. *Bloody Treason: on Solving History's Greatest Murder Mystery, the Assassination of John F. Kennedy*. Rancho Santa Fe, CA: Laurel Pub, 1997.

Waldron, Lamar, and Thom Hartmann. *Ultimate Sacrifice: John and Robert Kennedy, the Plan for a Coup in Cuba, and the Murder of JFK*. New York: Carroll & Graf, 2006.

Walker, Martin. *The Cold War: a History*. New York: H. Holt, 1995.

Wood III, Ira David. "The JFK Assassination Chronology: 19 January 1961 to 21 November 1963." *Assassination Research: Journal for the Advanced Study of the Death of JFK*, Volume 2 Number 1—2003: 1-131.

Zirbel, Craig I. *The Texas Connection: the Assassination of President John F. Kennedy*. Scottsdale, Ariz.: Texas Connection, 1991.

Notes

1   Horne, *Inside the Assassination Records Review Board*, Chapters 6, 8, 13.

2   Wood III, *The JFK Assassination Chronology*, Vol 2, No. 1, 2003. p2.

3   Ibid, 128.

4   Brugioni and McCort, *Eyeball to Eyeball*, 262.

5   Bird and Sherwin, *American Prometheus*, 309.

6   Carroll, *House of War,* 535, note 34.

7   Walker, *The Cold War,* 20.

8   Ibid.

9   Kohn and Harahan, *Strategic Air Warfare,* 88.

10   Rhodes, *Dark Sun,* 562.

11   Rosenberg, David Allen, and W. B. Moore *"Smoking Radiating Ruin at the End of Two Hours": Documents on American Plans for Nuclear War with the Soviet Union, 1954-55* International Security, Vol 6, No. 3. pp3-38.

12   Brugioni, and McCort, *Eyeball to Eyeball,* 46.

13   Kaplan, *The Wizards of Armageddon,* 134.

14   Newhouse, *War and Peace in the Nuclear Age,* 119.

15   Chang and Kornbluh, *The Cuban Missile Crisis, 1962,* xvii.

16   Kahn, *On Thermonuclear War,* 16.

17   Walker, *The Cold War,* 27.

18   Kenney, *15 Minutes.*

19   Kennedy may have been making reference to what was known as the *Business Plot*, which was an attempt by American financiers to overthrow FDR in 1934.

20   Dallek, *An Unfinished Life,* 353.

21   Burke, Arleigh, CNO, *Memorandum: Recommended Courses of Action in Laos,* 1961.

22   Schlesinger, *A Thousand Days,* 234.

23   Brinkley and Douglas, *Dean Acheson,* 127.

24   Kornbluh, *Bay of Pigs Declassified,* 8.

25   Ibid, 2.

26   Carroll, *House of War*, 258.

27   Brugioni, and McCort, *Eyeball to Eyeball*, 60.

28   Newman, *JFK and Vietnam*, 54.

29   Douglass, *JFK and the Unspeakable*, 12-13.

30   Frankenheimer's film was released in 1962. The 2000 DVD version of the movie includes this note in its "Special Features" under the title "Political Forces":

> "From the start, the filmmakers discovered the multi-headed nature of the United States government. They received full cooperation at the White House because President Kennedy and many of his staff had read and enjoyed the novel.
>
> Frankenheimer and his assistants received permission to tour Kennedy's living quarters, to film entrance scenes at the White House, and to stage the riot out front behind the Iron Gate.
>
> However, the Defense Department wasn't as amenable. The filmmakers were denied access to the Chairman of the Joint Chiefs of Staff unless the screenplay was submitted for Defense Department "consideration."
>
> Frankenheimer refused what he believed to be a covert brand of censorship."

31   Newman, *JFK and Vietnam*, 18.

32   Schlesinger, *A Thousand Days*, 338.

33   Brinkley and Douglas, *Dean Acheson,* 136.

34   Douglass, *JFK and the Unspeakable*, 100.

35   Schlesinger, *A Thousand Days*, 339.

36   Dallek, *An Unfinished Life*, 352.

37   During the accident at the Three Mile Island Nuclear Power Plant in the spring and summer of 1979, scientists were taking measurements in the surrounding Pennsylvania streams and farmland to determine if any radioactive material had escaped from the plant. To their rising alarm, radioactive isotopes were found in all of the samples taken downwind of the plant. But, when they found the exact same readings in all of the upwind samples too, they came to the realization that what they were

actually measuring was fallout from the 336 aboveground nuclear tests that began in 1945 and ended in 1963. [From the author's conversation with one of the aforementioned scientists.]

[38] Chang and Kornbluh, *The Cuban Missile Crisis, 1962*, 15.

[39] JFKL, *Press Conferences of President Kennedy*, News Conference 17, October 11, 1961, Question and Response Number 6.

[40] JFKL, *Press Conferences of President Kennedy*, News Conference 16, August 30, 1961, Question and Response Number 10.

[41] Perlstein, Rick. *Before the Storm: Barry Goldwater and the Unmaking of the American Consensus*. E-Book ed. New York, NY: National Books, A Member of the Perseus Book Group, 2009. Chapter 8, "Apocalyptics," paragraph 10.

[42] Johnson complained about being assigned to the trip saying "There will be a lot of shooting and I'll be in the middle of it. Why me?" Johnson's fear of gunfire also manifested itself on the night before the assassination when he tried to protect his friend John Connally by attempting to exchange the Governor's seat assignment with Senator Ralph Yarborough's. There are also reports that as Johnson's car was turning onto Elm Street in Dealey Plaza, he ducked down in his seat. He was ducking *before* the first shot was fired.

[43] Talbot, *Brothers*, 70.

[44] Schlesinger, *A Thousand Days*, 388.

[45] Galbraith, James K., *Did the U.S. Military Plan a Nuclear First Strike for 1963?*, The American Prospect, Number 19, Fall 1994. pp88-96.

[46] The enhanced program for additional fallout shelters announced by the president in his address on Berlin resulted in the production of a booklet published by the Defense Department that provided instructions for homeowners on building fallout shelters in their own back yards. (Schlesinger, op.cit. 685). Many thought that this cruelly gave the public a false sense of hope, because surviving the fallout was certainly a secondary concern to surviving the thermonuclear blast from a Soviet attack. However, this meeting makes clear that the proposed shelters were not necessarily intended to withstand a nuclear attack from the Russians; these were for us to take shelter from the fallout encircling the globe after our all-out attack on them.

[47] Sagan, Scott D., *SIOP-62: The Nuclear War Briefing to President Kennedy*. International Security, Vol. 12, No. 1, Summer 1987. pp22-51.

[48] The Associated Press, *Milwaukee Sentinel*, October 28, 1961, p2.

49   Bamford, *Body of Secrets*, 82

50   Ibid, 73.

51   Newman, *JFK and Vietnam*, 137-138.

52   Allyn, Bruce, James Blight, and David Welsch. *Essence of Revision: Moscow, Havana, and the Cuban Missile Crisis*. International Security Vol. 14, No. 3. Winter 1989-1990. pp147-148.

53   Kaplan, *The Wizards of Armageddon*, 305.

54   JFKL, *Press Conferences of President Kennedy*, News Conference 43, September 13, 1962, The President's opening statement.

55   Brugioni, and McCort, *Eyeball to Eyeball*,. 377.

56   Ibid, 469.

57   Naftali and Zelikow, *The Presidential Recordings: The Great Crises II*, 583-584.

58   Dallek, *An Unfinished Life*, 555.

59   Rhodes, *Dark Sun*, 572.

60   Brugioni, and McCort, *Eyeball to Eyeball*, 474.

61   Ibid, 484.

62   Rhodes, *Dark Sun*, 575.

63   Sagan, *The Limits of Safety*, 78-80.

64   Khrushchev, Crankshaw, and Talbott, *Khrushchev Remembers*, 498.

65   Sagan, *The Limits of Safety*, 135.

66   Brugioni, and McCort, *Eyeball to Eyeball*, 464.

67   Sagan, *The Limits of Safety*, 130.

68   Rhodes, *Dark Sun*, 575.

69   Ibid, notes to 575.

70   Schlesinger, *A Thousand Days*, 831.

71   Brugioni and McCort, *Eyeball to Eyeball*, 263.

72   John F. Kennedy Library Digital Archive. Radio and television interview: *After Two Years: A Conversation with the president*: unedited version: Part 1, 16 December 1962. Time 00:22:15 Digital Identifier: JFKWHA-150.

73   Neumann, *JFK and Vietnam*, 322.

74   Ibid.

75   Allyn, Bruce, James Blight, and David Welsch. *Essence of Revision: Moscow, Havana, and the Cuban Missile Crisis*. International Security Vol. 14, No. 3, Winter 1989-1990. pp156-159.

76   Hershberg, Jim. *Anatomy of a controversy: Anatoly F. Dobrynin's Meeting with Robert F. Kennedy Saturday 27 October, 1962*. The Cold War International History Project Bulletin, Issue 5, Spring 1995, p80.

77 Fursenko and Naftali, *One Hell of a Gamble*, 321 and Schlesinger, *A Thousand Days*, 835.

78 JFKL, *Press Conferences of President Kennedy*, News Conference 61, September 12, 1963, Question and Response Numbers 13 and 14.

79 Although it is now widely recognized that the work had help from his assistant, Ted Sorenson, the book's idea and its central theme were Kennedy's own.

80 Brugioni, and McCort, *Eyeball to Eyeball*, 510.

81 State Department Telegram, Control No. 19238, U.S. Ambassador Hare to Secretary of State Rusk, *Re: Department Telegram 445*, October 27, 1962.

82 Newman, *JFK and Vietnam*, 3-4.

83 It has always been observed that the men in the photographs appear to be too well groomed to be tramps. One is smirking noticeably, they are not handcuffed, and the officers guarding them are walking too far in front and behind for it to be a genuine arrest. No record of that arrest has ever been found, and to this day, the three men are officially unidentified.

84 Close examination of the series of photos reveals that all four men, the man in the suit and the three tramps, are making a conscious effort to avoid eye contact and deliberately not acknowledging one another's presence.

85 Osanic, Len, *The Col. L Fletcher Prouty Reference Site*, <http://www.prouty.org/>.

86 Mellen, *A Farewell to Justice*, 72.

87 Garrison, *A Heritage of Stone*, 98-99.

88 National Geographic DVD, *The Lost Kennedy Tapes: The Assassination*. Vivendi Entertainment International, 2009. Chapter 15 Time 1:25:46.

89 It was given that moniker by David Belin, Assistant Counsel to the Warren Commission, who used the circular logic that Oswald had to have killed the President because he killed Tippit to get away, and that killing Tippit shows that he had the capability of committing the assassination.

90 Drenas, William M. "Car #10 Where Are You?": *Officer Tippit Timeline. The Kennedy Assassination.* October 1998. <http://mcadams.posc.mu.edu/car10.htm>.

91 The United States House of Representatives.*The Final Assassinations Report: Report.* New York: Bantam, 1979. p58.

92 C. V. Clifton, "Memorandum of Conference with the president," December 27, 1962, Palm Beach, NSF: Clifton Box 345, JFKL.

93 During the Watergate scandal ten years later, President Nixon sent his Chief of Staff, Bob Haldeman, to see CIA Director Richard Helms to persuade him to help stop the FBI investigation. On tape we hear Nixon instructing Haldeman:

> "When you get in to see these people, say: "Look, the problem is that this will open the whole, the whole Bay of Pigs thing, and the president just feels that . . . ah, I mean, without going into the details of, of lying to them to the extent to say that there is no involvement. But, you can say, "This is sort of a comedy of errors, bizarre," without getting into it, "The President's belief is that this is going to open the whole Bay of Pigs thing up again. And, ah because ah these people are playing for, for keeps and that they should call the FBI in and we feel that . . . that we wish for the country, don't go any further into this case, period!"

Haldeman writes in his memoirs that the CIA Director's reaction to the message was extremely hostile:

> "Turmoil in the room. Helms, gripping the arms of his chair, leaning forward and shouting, 'The Bay of Pigs had nothing to do with this! I have no concern about the Bay of Pigs!'

> Silence. I just sat there. I was absolutely shocked by Helms' violent reaction. Again I wondered, what was such dynamite in the Bay of Pigs story?"

Haldeman came to the conclusion that the Bay of Pigs was a reference to the Kennedy assassination. But he never explains why Nixon would use the name of the 1961 invasion of Cuba as a reference to the Kennedy assassination in 1963. This author believes that this was a coded message to Helms that Nixon knew that the Kennedy assassination was intended to be used as a pretext for a new invasion of Cuba. Nixon was using this knowledge as leverage with the CIA to call-off the FBI. Note that despite his protests to Haldeman, Helms complied with Nixon's request.

94 NSA, *Communication Intelligence Report (CIR)* Dated 27 Nov 63.

95 Marrs, *Crossfire,* 31. The author agrees with what Mr. Marrs here relates as researcher Gary Shaw's belief that the pair was sending a signal to JFK to let him know who was responsible for his death. And this author believes that Mr. Shaw correctly identifies the man seen waving, commonly referred to as "the dark-complected man," as a particular anti-Castro Cuban who was known to the President and was someone he would have immediately recognized. However, where Mr. Shaw believes that the umbrella represents the "umbrella" of air support which Kennedy cancelled during the Bay of Pigs, this author believes the umbrella to represent "Appeasement," which LeMay and the rest of the Chiefs believed Kennedy committed during the Cuban Missile Crisis. The black umbrella being the symbol of Neville Chamberlin.

96 The activities of the two men described are documented in both the Zapruder film as well as a number of still photographs taken in Dealey Plaza after the shooting.

97 Coffey, *Iron Eagle*, 430.

98 Kelly, Bill, *"Was LeMay at Camp X on 11/22/63?"* JFKcountercoup, June 4, 2012 <http://jfkcountercoup.blogspot.com/2012/06/was-lemay-at-camp-x-on-112263.html>

99 Unedited version of tape recording of conversations aboard Air Force One taken during the flight home from Dallas November 22, 1963 discovered amongst the effects of the estate of Kennedy's Military Aide, General Chester V. Clifton. Any and all references to Curtis LeMay were edited out of the official version of these tapes which are stored in the LBJ Library.

100 Law, William, *In the Eye of History*, 35.

101 Talbot, *Brothers*, 252.

102 NSA, *Communication Intelligence Report (CIR)* Dated 27 Nov 63.

103 Fursenko and Naftali, *One Hell of a Gamble*, 347.

104 Ibid, 350.

105 Schlesinger, *Robert Kennedy and His Times*, 529 Footnote.

106 Walker, *The Cold War*, 177.

107 One of the more famous examples of this is the television commercial for the '64 LBJ campaign which implied that Barry Goldwater would be an irresponsible president. It only ran once, but it had a devastating effect on the Goldwater campaign. In fact, its impact is still studied today. To really appreciate it, you have to view it first hand, but to give the reader an idea of the substance, it went like this:

The black & white scene opens looking up at a four to five year old girl standing in a field of flowers on a bright sunny day. She is looking down at the daisy she is holding in her right hand, and we can hear her small voice counting the pedals as she picks them off with her left. When she counts up to nine she unexpectedly looks up, somewhat startled; and her image is suddenly frozen in that position. At the same time the sound of her voice is gradually supplanted by the rising sound of an adult male voice that begins to count down from nine. As this countdown proceeds, the camera slowly but steadily zooms in on the fixed image of the little girl's freckled face, so that by the time the countdown reaches zero, our field of view is completely filled by the darkness of the pupil of her right eye. Suddenly, a white flash engulfs the screen, and as it slowly fades, the now familiar mushroom cloud from a thermonuclear explosion forms, and the next voice we hear is Lyndon Johnson's saying:

> These are the stakes:
> To make a world in which all of God's
> children can live; or to go into the dark.
> We must either love each other,
> or we must die.

The screen then shows, and a voice-over reads aloud:

Vote for President Johnson on November 3.

[108] The Gulf of Tonkin Incident consisted of two naval engagements off the coast of North Vietnam in August 1964. The first occurred on August 2, 1964, when the destroyer USS Maddox, while on patrol, was fired on by three North Vietnamese Navy torpedo boats. A naval battle resulted, in which one US aircraft was damaged, the destroyer was hit by one artillery round, and the three North Vietnamese torpedo boats were damaged. There were six North Vietnamese killed, but no U.S. casualties. The second incident was claimed by the U.S. as another attack resulting in another sea battle on August 4. But instead, it was

later admitted, the episode may have resulted from misinterpretation of weather effects on the ship's radar and not an actual NVN Torpedo Boat attack. The outcome of these two incidents was Congress's passage of the *Gulf of Tonkin Resolution*, which granted President Lyndon B. Johnson unrestricted war powers to assist any Southeast Asian nation that was the target of "communist aggression."

[109] Goodwin, *Lyndon Johnson and the American Dream*, 357.

[110] Twyman, *Bloody Treason*, 828.

[111] Ibid.

[112] Fursenko and Naftali, *One Hell of a Gamble*, 345.

[113] Ibid, 350.

[114] McNamara, *The Fog of War*.

[115] New York Times, July 6, 2009, p1.

[116] Chang and Kornbluh, *The Cuban Missile Crisis, 1962*, xiii.

[117] McNamara, *The Fog of War*.

[118] Rhodes, *Dark Sun*, 576.